FROM:

TO:

DATE:

COZY white COTTAGE

Create Your Own *Cozy*

217

Create Your Own Cozy

Published in Nashville, Tennessee, by Thomas Nelson. Thomas Nelson is a registered trademark of HarperCollins Christian Publishing, Inc.

Illustrations by Sharon Montgomery

ISBN 978-1-4002-4353-2 (HC)

Printed in India

23 24 25 26 27 REP 10 9 8 7 6 5 4 3 2 1

COZY *white* COTTAGE

CREATE YOUR OWN *Cozy*

100 PRACTICAL WAYS TO LOVE YOUR HOME AND LIFE

LIZ MARIE GALVAN

THOMAS NELSON
Since 1798

For you, dear reader.

May you find your own version of cozy.

BARR-Co.

Contents

INTRODUCTION

What does *cozy* mean to you?

Cozy. If you've read my other books or followed me online, then you know that coziness defines the way I live and work and play. *Cozy* is a state of mind, a guiding force that has seeped into my very soul. It's helped me navigate hard seasons and more fully enjoy the good ones.

And that, my friend, is what I want for you. I wrote this book to help you make your life as cozy as possible, to define what *cozy* means to you, and to show you how to incorporate those principles into your life and home so that you can make it a haven for you and yours. So together, let's dive into these pages and one hundred ideas to make them personal and beloved to *you.*

The past few years have been difficult for all of us. Separation and sickness, unrest and uncertainty, division and dissension have left so many of us feeling the absolute opposite of cozy. Maybe this has been your first experience grappling with anxiety, fear, and uncertainty. Or, if you're like me, maybe those feelings aren't new for you. Perhaps those feelings have been your companions for many years.

Through life's ups and downs, I've learned some things that have helped me, like creating a sense of home. *Home* was knowing myself and what was cozy to me so I could bring it with me anywhere life would take me. And that cozy mindset is part of what carried my husband, Jose, and me through his military deployments, the frustration and hopelessness of infertility, the overwhelming grief of eleven miscarriages, and the uncertainty followed by the eventual joy of our adoption journey—our son, Cope. I'm not sure I'd still be here today without the anchor cozy gave me when I needed it most.

And that's what I want you to discover in this book. I want to help you embrace your own personal definition of *cozy*, discover what feels like home (and what doesn't!), and create your own restorative rhythms of work and play and rest that prioritize cozy year-round. That way, you can create your own respite to retreat to when life gets decidedly un-cozy. Within these one hundred tips are monthly Home Maintenance Checklists that will guide you to create your own kind of cozy (because checklists always help and I've done the hard work for you).

I know that my style and my home are not everyone's definition of *cozy*, but it is *mine*. I want to help you to find *your* own *cozy*, *your* own style—a filter you can use to make the right choices for you at home, with your family, for yourself, and for your goals. I want to help you create a haven for yourself and your family that refuels you in body, mind, and spirit. I hope it will look beautiful at the end, but more importantly, I hope that it *feels* just as beautiful. My prayer is that these one hundred cozy tips, actions, and inspirations will lead you home.

ŒUVRES
P. CORNEILLE.
TOME IX.
ŒUVRES
P. CORNEILLE.

STRONG The Artist & the Garden

No. 01 What Does Cozy Mean to You?

Cozy is more than how a room looks or what's in it; it's how the room functions, how it triggers each of your five senses, and how it comes together in a way that is comforting and peaceful to you.

My cozy recipe is mixing the old with the new. I like the comfort and ease of new technology and "easy to live with and wash" textiles. But I pair that with antiques and the vintage décor I'm known for on my blog and in my shop. That mix of old and new allows me to choose pieces that function well for my family and still look beautiful to me. I choose items that fit my style—even utilitarian things like a broom, a bottle of cleaning spray, and our television.

For me, my senses need to be aligned and at peace for a space to feel cozy. Everything can look beautiful, but if the furniture feels stiff, a musty smell lingers in the air, or an annoying noise hums along in the background, I won't feel cozy. I need what I see, smell, touch, and hear to be in harmony, which means soft, warm light; comfy seats for lounging and snuggling; the sight of a snoozing pet; a fresh scent in the air; and (usually) the sounds of Jose and Cope nearby. That's cozy magic. It doesn't hurt if there's also something delicious to snack on!

Now let's discover *your* definition of *cozy*.

When it comes to feeling cozy in your home, what is the most important sense to you?

....

....

....

....
....
....
....
....
....

Think about a time you felt the coziest in your space. What did the room look like? Smell like? Feel like? Sound like?

....
....
....
....
....
....
....
....

Picture the coziest space you can think of. What does it look like? Describe it in detail.

....
....
....
....
....
....
....
....
....

NO. 02 Why Cozy Matters

We all need a safe, comforting place to land. Somewhere we can regroup, heal, and feel all of our big feelings without worrying about being judged or laughed at or let down. I need a cozy space to call my own for my mental health, and I'll bet that you do too.

Cozy is an important feeling to create in our spaces so that our homes can be an oasis to all those who dwell there. Your home should be a haven. Creating rooms and rhythms and a way of living that is cozy and welcoming is a gift that you give yourself and your family. Home should have a way of hugging you when you walk through the front door. It should be a place where you can lay down your stresses and find peace. It should be the place where everyone who lives there can be their most comfortable, authentic, peace-filled selves.

Creating rooms and rhythms and a way of living that is cozy and welcoming is a gift that you give yourself and your family.

It doesn't matter if your idea of cozy and my idea of cozy have nothing in common. Cozy can be accomplished in any style and on any budget. Your home doesn't have to be fully renovated and magazine-worthy to be a cozy refuge for your family. The world outside your walls can be ugly and cruel, but we can each create our own little world under our roofs where we can gather with our families to thank God and be blessed.

Cozy Tip

Always leave a light on until everyone is home safe and sound for the night. There is something so comforting about seeing that golden glow through the windows welcoming you home.

No. 03 What Does Cozy Mean to Your People?

You can't create a cozy haven until you understand what makes something cozy for you. This is more than just your style—although that's part of it!

For a home to truly be cozy, it must be cozy for *everyone* who lives there. Ask these questions to get a better idea of what *cozy* means to them.

Describe the most recent time you felt cozy.

When you have a bad day, what sounds most comforting to you?

What's your favorite smell?

Is there a place in the house where you don't enjoy spending time? Why?

What's your favorite way for all of us to spend time together? Why?

What's your favorite meal? Why do you like it so much?

What's the comfiest place to lounge? Why?

Close your eyes and describe the coziest place you can imagine. What makes it so cozy?

Of the people you know, whose home do you find the coziest? Who is the coziest person you know? Why did you pick that person?

Who is the best host or hostess you know? Why does their home feel welcoming to you?

What's the cozy thing they do that you'd never have thought to do yourself?

When you were growing up, whose home made you feel safe and welcome? Why?

NO. 04 *Cozy* Starts with You

I confess there are times, despite how cozy my home is, that I don't feel cozy at all. Almost every single time that happens, it's because I haven't been taking care of myself. I've been running myself ragged, burning the candle at both ends, eating junk that doesn't nourish my body, and generally putting myself last on the list.

Yikes, right? I would never treat anyone else in my life that way, but I've done it way too often to myself without a second thought. Luckily, since embracing cozy as a way of life, I've gotten much better at intentionally and lovingly taking care of myself, just like I do with my home and my family. A lot of people hear *self-care*

Choosing the right ways for you and making those things a priority will give you a cozy feeling that nothing store-bought ever will.

---

and think of going to a spa or taking a bubble bath. Those things certainly *can be* self-care, but usually it's bigger than that. *Self-care* means caring for your whole self the best way you can. It's nourishing your body with good food, exercise, and plenty of sleep. It means having practices like prayer and worship to nourish your soul, reading good books and meditating to nourish your mind, and spending time in nature and on hobbies that nourish your mental health.

Like creating a cozy room, creating a self-care routine will look different for each of us depending on what we need most. While eating junk food generally makes me feel worse, there are times when treating myself to a cupcake is the coziest thing I can think of! Self-care for you may be a big bowl of mac and cheese, or if you haven't been eating well, it may be a salad brimming with fresh veggies.

And self-care won't always look the same during different seasons of your life. Everyone needs a good night's sleep, but if you are a mama with a newborn, a nap is probably the best gift you can give to yourself. If you have older kids with busy schedules, self-care may be ordering in dinner so you can spend your precious downtime connecting with your kids instead of cooking for them. Busy working on your career? Self-care may be taking a seminar to grow your skills or starting a side hustle to help you gain experience.

There are many different ways to care for ourselves. Choosing the right ways for you and making those things a priority will give you a cozy feeling that nothing store-bought ever will.

No. 05 Cozy Rhythms

In so many ways, farm life has taught me how to slow down and find rhythms that work for our family. When you share your life with a wide assortment of animals, it really shows you that busyness and urgency are human inventions. Chickens don't feel guilty for taking a midday nap. Lambs don't feel the need to say *yes* to everything and make sure they're doing *enough*. No, they listen to their bodies; they eat when they're hungry and rest when they're tired. Lambs spend their days running and playing through the fields and spend their nights snuggling and sleeping without a care. We can learn a lot from them.

My tomato plants don't cling to summer or refuse to move on to fall. I can't make the sun shine or the rain come or make a single plant grow faster. The same is true for my little family.

I can't keep Cope a little boy forever or magically add hours to my day. But what I *can* do is embrace the season I'm in. I can focus on being fully present for the moments that matter. And I can learn to say *no* to the things that aren't important so I can say *yes*

Yes to hours of playtime and art projects with my little one, *yes* to long afternoons digging in the garden because it brings me joy, and *yes* to time spent on DIY projects with my husband, laughing ourselves silly when we mess up.

to the things that are. *Yes* to hours of playtime and art projects with my little one, *yes* to long afternoons digging in the garden because it brings me joy, and *yes* to time spent on DIY projects with my husband, laughing ourselves silly when we mess up.

What does your family need most right now? Really think about what's essential for each member of your family. How can you prioritize those things? What are you doing that isn't as important as you thought? How can you gracefully bow out of it?

Each season of the year and each season of your life will bring new challenges and new priorities. Be flexible and know that you'll need to adjust as you go along. Keep choosing the cozy rhythms that fill your home with laughter, peace, and love over the stressful schedules that create chaos without fostering connection. The more you do it, the easier it gets. And the reward of a cozier life for you and yours is worth the extra effort.

No. 06 Cozy Goals

Whether you want a cozier home, more comfortable and supportive relationships, or a calmer and more peace-filled lifestyle, you won't create it by accident. *Cozy* isn't something that happens to you; it's something you create, little by little, choice by choice.

If you want a cozy life, you must go after it with intention. Set goals for yourself and start working toward them. Here are a few questions to get you started.

What is cozy about your life right now?

....

....

Could it be cozier? How?

....

....

How would your friends describe your life? Dramatic? Calm? Aspirational? Messy? Are those descriptions close to cozy or far away?

....

....

Do people enjoy spending time in your home? Why or why not?

....

....

Do *you* enjoy spending time in your home? Why or why not?

....

....

....

Are you happy with your current routines and schedule? What do you like and dislike?

....

....

....

What are you most thankful for about your life? Relationships? Home?

....

....

....

How could those things be better?

....

....

....

Set three small cozy goals for the next one hundred days:

1. ....
2. ....
3. ....

Set three big cozy goals for the year ahead:

1. ....
2. ....
3. ....

No. 07 Action Items

I'm a firm believer in breaking down bigger projects into smaller steps and taking them a little at a time. I'm also a firm believer in not waiting for things to be finished to make them cozy. Life has many seasons of waiting. Waiting for the next step in your job, to find the perfect partner, for the baby you've been praying for, or to save the money to tackle a home project. Let's make the best of the wait. *Cozy* is more than just an end goal; it's a process that can be curated every step of the way.

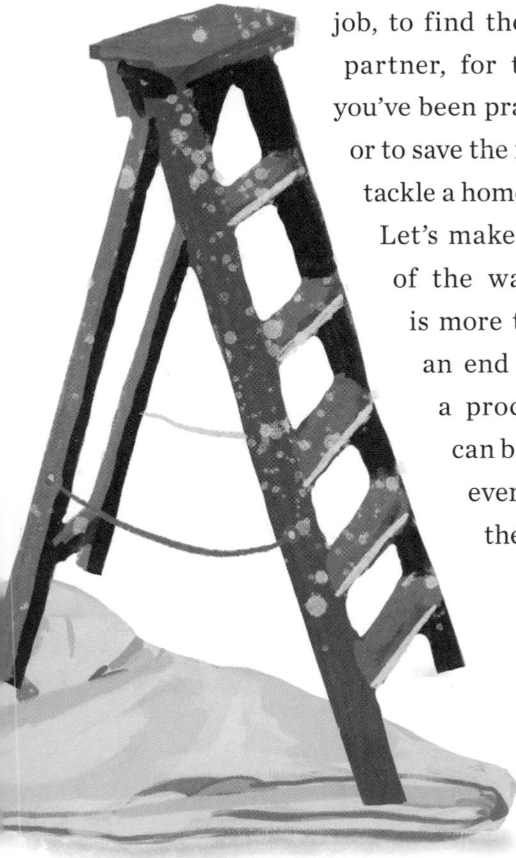

When we purchased our farmhouse, there were more projects in front of us than we could list, let alone tackle right away. But I didn't let that stop me from starting where I was with what I had. Our kitchen, for example, was dark and unwelcoming and needed a complete overhaul. We didn't have the money to do that right away. But we did have the money for a few cans of white paint and some inexpensive paneling to cover the dated stone wall treatments. It was far from finished, but those first small steps made the kitchen so much cozier!

You don't have to wait for everything to align to get started. In fact, taking the first small steps has a way of making the bigger steps feel more doable. Go back to your Cozy Goals from pages 16 and 17. Pick a biggie. Now break it down into action steps.

What will need to be done first?

....

....

....

Are there steps that rely on other things being done first? What are the steps and the timelines for *those* things?

....

....

....

Which parts of this project can you do yourself? Where will you need help? What kind of help will you need?

....

....

....

What are the timeline and budget for this project?

....

....

....

What can you afford or have time to do right away to make it cozier?

....

....

....

Go do the little things to make it cozier until you can complete the project the way you want. I promise it will be worth it!

No. 08 January Home Maintenance Checklist

Homes, like people, require care to remain healthy and happy. It's tough to feel cozy when you have a leak in your ceiling because you forgot to clean your gutters! Spreading your checklists out across the year makes it easier to stay on top of things. I've included monthly lists to get you started and have left room for you to add tasks specific to your family and home. You'll see that I include "freshening up" on each month's list because I like to start each season with a clean slate. Feel free to use the boxes on the right as a checklist for years to come.

JANUARY HOME MAINTENANCE CHECKLIST						
	Clean and put away Christmas or other holiday decorations. Fix any burnt-out lights or purchase discounted replacements for deteriorating decorations.					
	Freshen up your décor. Once Christmas is packed away, my house always looks a little empty, and I like to add more winter elements to keep it cozy. I love cozy textures, twinkle lights, evergreens, and candles.					
	Organize, clean out, and pack away Christmas wrapping supplies.					
	Find homes for new Christmas gifts; this may include donating some.					
	Touch up paint around your home.					
	Oil indoor door hinges, locks, and handles to keep them working smoothly.					

	Flush out your water heater to remove sediment buildup to make sure you have plenty of hot water during the cold months ahead.						
	Give your refrigerator and freezer a good scrub, both inside and outside. Remove any expired or unused food and condiments.						
	Clean out your pantry. Toss expired items, donate items you won't be using to a food bank, and get yourself organized for a new year of cooking and baking.						
	Plan for the year ahead. Go room by room and identify small and big projects you'd like to tackle for the year. Set a budget, gather inspiration, and start researching so you can buy them at the best possible price. Your future self will thank you!						
	Clean the garbage disposal at least once a month to keep it from getting moldy and smelly. Remove the rubber splash guard and scrub it well. Pour half a cup of baking soda into the disposal and let it sit for thirty minutes. Add one cup of vinegar and let that sit for five minutes. Rinse the disposal out with hot water from the tap. Add two cups of ice and a heavy sprinkling of kosher salt, and grind until processed. This will keep your blades nice and sharp. In between cleanings, if you notice an odor, throw in half a lemon and grind well. It will help reduce odor buildup and make your whole kitchen smell lemony fresh.						
	Check your HVAC filters and change them as needed. These should be changed every one to two months, but during high pollen season, you may need to change them more frequently. Pro tip: set a "subscribe and save" order for these through your favorite online retailer. I check my filters and replace them the day the new filters arrive.						

	Vacuum your dryer's lint trap. Removing lint from the trap between each round of drying helps, but it's impossible to get all the lint without the help of a vacuum. Use the smallest attachment you have to really get down into the lint trap and suck up as much as you can. Dryer lint is one of the most common fire starters in homes, so this is an important safety precaution that also keeps your dryer working well.						
	If you have a water softener system, check it once a month for salt bridges, mushing, and to see if it needs additional salt. It only takes five minutes to keep these systems running smoothly, but it takes a lot more time (and money!) to fix them if something goes wrong.						
	Check the temperature on your water heater and its pressure relief valves once a month. To do this, lift the pressure relief valve. If water doesn't come out instantly, you know it's time to replace this valve. You'll also want to check for any leaks or cracks. This is especially important if you have an older water heater. They generally last between ten and twelve years. If yours is older than that, it may be time to start saving for a replacement.						
	If you have pets, give them their monthly flea, tick, and heart guard medicines.						

No. 09 Knowing Your Measurements

Creating a cozy, beautiful home takes time. That's why it's so important to have measurements on hand for the different rooms and spaces in your home. When you stumble on the perfect buffet for your dining room, you'll be able to quickly figure out if it will fit on that empty wall. Or when you find a woven basket at a bargain price, you'll be able to see if it will fit on your empty shelves. Knowing your room's dimensions will also come in handy when you try to figure out furniture arrangements, find rugs, and even how many lamps you need for a space.

I've created a Cozy Home Guide in the back of this book to keep track of measurements and other essential information to make shopping for your home much easier and more joyful. Grab a heavy-duty measuring tape, and turn to page 210 to jot down your measurements. But before you do, I have a few tips to make this process easier.

1. Ask a friend or two for help. It's nearly impossible to hold a measuring tape in the right place and read it for an accurate measurement, especially if it's covering a longer distance.
2. For measuring longer distances, use a level to ensure your measuring tape is straight so you can get an accurate measurement.
3. When measuring windows or doorways, note if you are measuring only the opening itself or including the trim.
4. Bring your stud finder along and note how close the studs are in the walls of each room. This will be important for hanging art, mirrors, signs, or mounting televisions or floating shelves. A large piece may not work in your space if it needs to be centered and there isn't a stud handy.
5. If you're decorating a room from scratch, it helps to sketch out a floorplan using graph paper once you have all your measurements in hand. That way

you can draw different furniture placements to get a feel for scale before you buy that oversized chair. If hand-drawing isn't your thing, there are a lot of apps and software programs that allow you to do this digitally. We love to use SketchUp. As a bonus, you can keep your plans on your phone so you always have them with you when you're shopping.

6. Don't forget to measure your outdoor spaces like patios, porches, and decks. They are part of your living space too!

No. 10
Finding the Existing Cozy

Chances are you already have some cozy things in your home. A supersoft blanket. A cozy corner for reading with a comfy chair and a just-the-right-level-of-brightness lamp. A soup bowl that fits perfectly in your hand. A beautiful flower bed that you enjoy tending. Whatever those places are for you, they are important information to help you define what *cozy* means to you.

Go outside and take a short walk around the block, then come back to your home with fresh eyes. Walk around, both inside and outside. Look at everything and identify what already works for you, what already makes you feel cozy. These things are the starting points.

Do you like the layout of your rooms? Be specific about what you like and dislike.

....

....

....

Which of your paint colors do you like? Which do you dislike? Why?

....

....

....

Which rooms feel dysfunctional?

....

....

....

How can your rooms work better for you? A different layout? More aesthetically pleasing elements? More light or different furniture?

....

....

Which room do you want to spend more time in than others?

....

....

Do you like the look of your furniture? The feel of it?

....

....

....

Do you have enough storage? Where do you need more?

....

....

....

Which pieces of art and décor make you feel happy when you look at them?

....

....

....

What do you like best about those things?

....

....

....

What colors do you like in your décor? Are there some you don't like?

....

....

....

No. 11 Your Cozy Style Quiz

A big part of feeling cozy in your space is decorating it in your style. We all feel more inspired when we're surrounded by what's beautiful to us, which is essentially our style. There are a lot of different styles out there and fewer rules than you might think. The only design rule I put any stock in is to fill your home with things that make you feel happy and cozy. You can mix styles, patterns, colors, and decades however you like, as long as it feels right to you.

That said, most people find it helpful to create a name for their style so they can make decisions and purchases that feel cohesive and harmonious. This can be any mix of words that helps you picture your style clearly in your mind.

I'd describe my style as "cozy white cottage farmhouse." When I close my eyes and say that aloud, it makes me think of vintage, well-loved pieces combined with lots of white and wood and terracotta and natural materials like linen and woven baskets. I see a little stone cottage or an old farmhouse with a big porch. It conjures up warm, glowing lights; and plants and flowers; and warm breezes through open windows and doors. It's a little old-fashioned, a little playful, and a lot romantic.

Find Your Style

- Bohemian
- Danish Modern
- Mid-Century Modern
- Scandinavian
- Victorian
- Farmhouse
- Cottagecore
- Traditional
- Industrial

Look around your home. How would you describe the style of your décor?

....

....

....

Your furniture?

....

....

The architecture of the building itself?

....

....

....

....

Is this what you want it to be?

....

....

....

....

Do each of your rooms feel right to you? Do you feel you belong?

....

....

....

....

What styles are you most drawn to when you look at blogs, social media accounts, or magazines?

....

....

....

What style, would you say, are the rooms where you'd want to move right in?

....

....

....

How would you describe what you would buy for your home if you had an unlimited budget?

....

....

Now, create a name for your style. Sit with it a while and make sure it fits. You can always come back and change it if it doesn't. There is no right or wrong answer, so take your time until the words come together in a way that feels *just right* to you.

....

....

No. 12 Keeping It Cozy

Sometimes what you *don't* want is as important as what you *do*. If you're struggling to figure out what *cozy* is for you, you may have more luck by figuring out what it isn't. I'm sure at some point you've walked into a space that was decidedly *not* cozy to you, right? There's usually a reason for that. Identify what repels you so you can find and remove those items and not purchase things like them again.

What are some décor items or trends that are really *un*-cozy to you?

....

....

What colors do you dislike?

....

....

Which trends are you already over?

....

....

What kinds of materials (like tile or carpeting) do you not want in your home?

....

....

Things that are a bit more subtle may be making your home feel less than cozy too. Has it had a good, deep cleaning lately? Give everything a good scrub. Is there too much clutter? Then it's time to edit and organize

what you have. Keep what you love, donate what you can, and toss the rest. Are there unfinished projects everywhere you look? Which one is easiest to tackle? Start there. Are you stuck with inherited furniture or hand-me-down items that you don't actually love but feel too guilty to get rid of? Can you DIY them to be more your style or offer those items to other family members who may love them? Do you have areas you are unhappy with but aren't ready to fully renovate? Might be time for a mini-project to make those areas cozy until you can really tackle them.

Ignoring those things won't get you any closer to cozy. Instead, it's time to deal with them. Take some time to walk around and pinpoint what is really bothering you in your space.

How can you address those issues?

....

....

....

....

....

No. 13 Where to Start

If your whole home is feeling less than cozy, I suggest starting with the areas in your home that you use the most. Whenever we moved into a new home, we always started with the kitchen, which is the heart of the home for us, and then moved on to the living room or dining room. The rooms we don't spend as much time in go last on the list.

Another important consideration as you start is your budget. Prioritize spending your money where it will make the biggest impact. Sometimes that means waiting patiently until you can afford what you want. Other times, it may mean addressing something in a temporary way until you have the money to make a permanent change.

When we moved into our current home, there was old, filthy, wall-to-wall carpet in every room—even the bathrooms! We didn't have the money in our budget to lay down hardwood flooring, but we couldn't live with that carpet. So, we got creative. Pine boards were inexpensive at the time, so we laid those down and gave them a coat of inexpensive white deck paint, and we've lived with that for more than six years. Was it perfect? No. But did it make our home instantly cleaner and cozier? Yes! Now, we are slowly updating the flooring when we tackle each room and finding new uses for those old pine boards, like using them to build a chicken coop!

I don't recommend sacrificing your long-term renovations or savings goals for a want. But if you have a need, consider finding a cozy way to address it.

It's taken us years to get our farmhouse to where it is now, and it will take years more to get it even close to finished. We take things one day and one room at a time, prioritizing the spaces we need and tackling the projects that give us the biggest cozy return on our investments. In the meantime, we make smaller changes and updates to get us through until we can get to the big stuff. We are all works in progress. Start where you are—just as long as you start!

What is the greatest need that you have?

....
....
....
....
....
....
....

What is in your budget right now?

....
....
....
....
....
....
....

What temporary, affordable changes can you make until your budget and time allow you to tackle that project?

....
....
....
....
....
....
....

No. 14 Creating Home Shopping Lists

I love to shop for my home, especially at antique and thrift shops. There's so much hidden treasure out there waiting to be found. However, it's easy to fall into shopping pitfalls: buying too much stuff or wanting something so specific it's frustrating when I can't find it. Here are my tips to make the most of your shopping experiences:

1. Fill out all the sections of this book, especially the Cozy Home Guide section in the back. You'll be prompted to record your home's measurements, paint colors, fabric info, and finishes so that you have it all in one place. This will make shopping much easier!
2. Have a plan but hold it loosely. If you know you need seating to fill a certain amount of space, by all means, look for the sofa of your dreams. But if you discover a loveseat and chair combo that will look great and fits your budget, be open to exploring that option too. Stay a little flexible, and you may just find something better than you ever expected.
3. Have specific parameters without too many limitations. Do you need a vintage sign? Or do you need a vintage sign that is 12 x 12 inches in shades of blue or green that will work thematically in a laundry room?
4. Be patient. The only thing worse than not finding anything to buy is buying something out of desperation, only to get it home and realize you shouldn't have wasted your money.
5. Be spontaneous. You never know where you'll find that perfect piece, so take ten minutes to look around if you pass an antique shop or thrift store.
6. No regrets. If it's not a *heck yes*, then it's a *no*. I won't make my home cozier by filling it with things I don't love. Hold out for the best items.

OLDE SALT • Virginia • Briny
OTTER COVE • Washington • Sweet
OYSTERPONDS • Long Island • Mild
OYSTERVILLE SELECT • Washington • Sweet
PACIFIC ORCHARD • British Columbia • Sweet
PARAMOUR • Chesapeake Bay • Mild
PEACOCK COVE • New Brunswick • Mild
PEALE PASSAGE • Puget Sound • Sweet
PEARL BAY • British Columbia • Sweet
PEARL POINT • Tillamook • Sweet
PEBBLE BEACH • South Hood Canal • Sweet
PECONIC BAY • Long Island • Mild
PEMAQUID • Damariscotta River • Briny
PENN COVE SELECT • Puget Sound • Sweet
SALUTATION COVE • Prince Edward Island • Briny
SAMISH BAY • Northern Puget Sound • Sweet
SHIP'S POINT • Vancouver Island • Sweet
SINKU • British Columbia • Sweet
SISTER POINT • South Hood Canal • Sweet
SKOOKUM • Hood Canal • Sweet
SNOW CREEK • Northern Puget Sound • Sweet
SNOW HILL • Virginia • Mild
SPINNEY CREEK • Maine • Mild
STEAMBOAT • South Hood Canal • Sweet
STELLAR BAY • Vancouver Island • Sweet
STINGRAY • Chesapeake Bay • Sweet, Medium Briny
SUMMER ICE • British Columbia • Sweet
SUMMERSIDE • Prince Edward Island • Briny
SUN HOLLOW • Lower Hood Canal • Sweet
SUNSET BEACH • South Hood Canal • Sweet
SWEET NECK • Martha's Vineyard • Mild
TARGET ROCK • Long Island • Mild
MIRRO
MATIC

No. 15 Shop Tracker

If you only shop at big-box stores, you'll miss out on so many amazing treasures for your home. There are amazing locally owned shops in your area that are worth visiting and have a more varied inventory. The more you go, the more you'll get a feel for which shops carry stuff you always want to buy, when each store has sales and special deals, and when they get new deliveries in stock.

These days, there are more shopping options available than ever—you can even purchase items right from social media. I follow all my favorite shops on social media, so I always know when they update their inventory or have sales. I use the Folders option in Instagram and Pinterest to organize them so I can find what I want when I'm ready to shop. For example, I have a folder labeled "Local Small Shops" and another labeled "Shops I Want to Visit" and one that's labeled "Favorite Shops."

My Favorite Shops

SHOP NAME: ....
Address: ....
Phone Number: ....
Website: ....
Hours: ....
Best days to shop: ....
Notes: ....

SHOP NAME: ....
Address: ....
Phone Number: ....
Website: ....
Hours: ....
Best days to shop: ....
Notes: ....

SHOP NAME: ....
Address: ....
Phone Number: ....
Website: ....
Hours: ....
Best days to shop: ....
Notes: ....

SHOP NAME: ....
Address: ....
Phone Number: ....
Website: ....
Hours: ....
Best days to shop: ....
Notes: ....

SHOP NAME: ....
Address: ....
Phone Number: ....
Website: ....
Hours: ....
Best days to shop: ....
Notes: ....

SHOP NAME: ....
Address: ....
Phone Number: ....
Website: ....
Hours: ....
Best days to shop: ....
Notes: ....

SHOP NAME: ....
Address: ....
Phone Number: ....
Website: ....
Hours: ....
Best days to shop: ....
Notes: ....

SHOP NAME: ....
Address: ....
Phone Number: ....
Website: ....
Hours: ....
Best days to shop: ....
Notes: ....

No. 16 Mood Boards

Mood boards help me put all my thoughts together in one place and give me insight I might miss otherwise. Taking a little extra time to create a mood board gives me a lens to make decisions so I am much more likely to curate a space I really love.

When it comes to building mood boards, I'm a big fan of the old-fashioned, cut-and-paste method using paint samples, pictures cut from magazines and catalogs, and fabric swatches. Then I layer on photos of the big stuff—furniture, light fixtures, an important piece of wall décor, paint samples, and fabric swatches. Whenever I can, I try to cut pictures to show only whatever element I'm interested in. After that, I add the smaller touches—more art, throw pillow options, inspiration. By the time I'm finished, I have a much better idea for how I want the room to look *and* feel.

If cutting and pasting and digital editing feels too daunting, I recommend heading over to Pinterest. Create a board for your room and then start pinning pictures that feel right. It's not exactly the same as a mood board, but creating a Pinterest board will allow you to get a clearer idea of what you are drawn to and to spot patterns that can help you make decisions.

If something isn't working on the board, remove and replace until the board feels perfectly cozy.

Digital Mood Boards

I also like creating digital mood boards. Programs and apps like AdobeExpress, Canva, Spoak, and Shuffles by Pinterest make it easy to erase backgrounds and trim digital images and put them together. I even take photos of my existing furniture and décor and incorporate them onto the mood board, if those pieces are going to stay in the room.

NO. 17 CREATE A MOOD BOARD

Now it's your turn to make a mood board for the coziest version of your home!

Let's start with the overall cozy vibe you'd like to create. Go through magazines and catalogs to find photos that match the feel you're after. Pick up some paint samples or fabric swatches from local shops.

Then use this space to tape or glue everything in. If you need more space or want to create mood boards for specific rooms, use the blank pages at the back of this book. Once you are finished, take a step back and look at what you've created. What patterns are you noticing? Is there a common thread that can help you make future decisions for your home?

NO. 18 Go Custom

Sometimes the coziest solutions for our home are custom ones. This doesn't always mean DIY, although it absolutely can, and it doesn't have to mean expensive either. There are affordable custom options, and some DIYs only need a little paint and elbow grease, which is about as inexpensive as it gets.

Not everything can be customized easily, but lots of the basics can be. And you'll end up with a piece you have a little extra love for because you helped create it.

- Building furniture: It's easier than ever to build a piece of custom furniture for your home. Lots of builders offer free or inexpensive plans online that you can download and print. This option will require some bigger power tools, and I highly recommend starting with simpler options like coffee tables or shelves before moving onto advanced projects like armoires or dressers. Of course, you can always hire someone to build a piece for you, if doing it yourself seems too difficult.

  Pros: You can create exactly what you want from high-quality materials and customize every aspect of the design.

  Cons: Building furniture isn't easy, and it takes practice to get good. It's also more time consuming than other options.

- Redoing furniture: Swapping out knobs or feet on tables and dressers can give an old piece a whole new vibe. Or, you can go all in and strip off old paint and stain, sand your piece, and refinish it with new stain or paint. I love pieces that feature both paint and stain. There's something about that combo that always works for me!

  Pros: You can get high-quality, solid-wood pieces for a fraction of the price of new, flimsier options if you are willing to refinish them.

  Cons: Stripping furniture is tough, stinky work that takes some time, so plan accordingly.

- Reusing antiques: An old dresser or store counter can be reused in unexpected ways (think of a kitchen island or a bathroom vanity) to prolong its life. This gives you a high-end custom look for a lower price.
- Caning: Caning is an art form that adds so much visual interest and texture to furniture. It's not something you can DIY from scratch—you'll have to hire an expert. However, you can faux DIY this! Hardware stores sell pre-made caning panels you can inset into cabinet doors or drawer fronts for a fresh update to a tired old piece.

NO. 19 Cozy Fabrics and Textiles

Fabrics and textiles can make all the difference in creating the perfect cozy spaces. Here are a few key elements to consider as you add to your décor.

- Draperies: Draperies can really eat into your budget, but a basic drapery panel is a simple rectangle with a hem on each side. You can easily make them yourself! A hem is just a nice, straight line that is pretty easy to master even for a beginner on an inexpensive machine. Or, you can do what I do and use iron-on hem tape! If you don't feel confident enough to try this one, check out your local dry cleaner or tailor. Many will sew hems for very reasonable prices.

  Pros: You can choose your fabric, length, and finishing options for a completely custom look.

  Cons: You may need to get a sewing machine.

- Throw pillow covers: Creating your own throw pillow covers requires a little more advanced sewing, but it is so worth it. I love having this option because it allows me to turn my favorite vintage textiles into throw pillows. Tea towels, scarves, and quilts can all be repurposed with a little thread and stuffing! Sewing is a struggle for me, so I ask my mother-in-law for help with pillows.

  Pros: You can turn any fabric into a pillow!

  Cons: A sewing machine is required. Hem tape won't work for this one!

- Upholstery: It's pretty simple to change out the fabric on the seats of dining room chairs or the top of an ottoman, but there is a real art to upholstering anything more complicated. A good upholsterer is worth every penny to

take a tired old chair with good bones and turn it into a showstopper with help from new fabric and extra stuffing.

Pros: New upholstery breathes new life into old pieces and can allow you to truly customize your furniture.

Cons: A good upholsterer can be tough to find, and this option isn't always budget-friendly.

- Slipcovers: I always try to get a neutral slipcover made for my upholstered furniture. This gives me a custom look that is easy to clean. If you are looking for someone who can sew slipcovers, visit your local fabric store and ask the friendly folks who work there. Chances are, they know everyone in town who sews and can make a recommendation!

Pros: Slipcovers prolong the life of your furniture and let you change up your look for less.

Cons: It can be a challenge to find someone who can make one.

- Knitting and Crochet: Knitted or crocheted blankets, pillow covers, table runners, and even plant hangers can add so much coziness to a room. If you are crafty and want to learn, you can easily make these yourself.

No. 20 February Home Maintenance Checklist

By February, the excitement of Christmas and New Year has faded away, and we are deep into winter and snow in Michigan. This is the month when we spend the most time indoors, which makes it the perfect time to do more home editing and organizing to reduce clutter and keep our home feeling cozy. It's also the time of year I like to curl up and dream about the spring to come.

FEBRUARY HOME MAINTENANCE CHECKLIST						
	Clean out the whole family's colder weather wardrobes. Remove pieces that are damaged, don't fit, or never get used. This includes activewear, underthings, socks, and pajamas. Donate anything still in useable condition.					
	Clean out your medicine cabinets. Responsibly dispose of expired or unneeded medication using the instructions on www.FDA.gov. Dispose of expired or no longer used beauty and self-care products.					
	Assess your backstock of frequently used items and stock up as needed. This should include things like toothbrushes, toothpaste, shampoo, conditioner, bodywash, soap, laundry detergent, and other essentials so that you never run out in the middle of a blizzard.					
	Reorganize and clean out toys, pots and pans, bakeware, small appliances, and other items you may have a surplus of.					

	If needed, restock firewood and give your fireplace a gentle cleaning.						
	Plan ahead for warmer months. Need to update landscaping? Research plant options and be ready to purchase plants and seeds when it's warm enough. Plot your kitchen or herb garden based on what grows best for when (and what) you like to eat. Order seeds ahead so you can start finicky plants indoors and transfer them to the garden when the time is right.						
	Clean up garlands that have gone from fresh to dried. When you get the winter blues, replace them with a few happy new plants from your local nursery to serve as a reminder that spring is coming.						
	Clean the garbage disposal.						
	Check your HVAC filters and change them as needed.						
	Vacuum your dryer's lint trap.						
	Check your water softener system.						
	Check the temperature on your water heater.						
	If you have pets, give them their monthly flea, tick, and heart guard medicines.						

No. 21 Cozy and Kindness

For me, *cozy* and *kindness* go hand in hand. Cozy people are kind people who treat others well and build community that welcomes everyone in. That kind of cozy kindness starts with being kind to yourself.

If you are beating yourself up for every mistake, holding yourself to unreasonable expectations, and working yourself to exhaustion, how can you possibly have the internal resources left to treat others well? If we want to be able to be kind to others, we must first be kind to ourselves.

For many of us, this may be the biggest challenge in this book. If that's you, I see you, and I understand. And I promise that it is possible to change the habits of a lifetime and learn to know and love yourself for exactly who you are. Imagine what you could accomplish if you treated yourself with the same level of kindness and care with which you treat your favorite people.

When I'm being less than kind to myself, my response is to lean into cozy. It's difficult to be hard on yourself when you are busy being kind to yourself instead. Light your favorite candles and relax in a bubble bath. Make your favorite comfort food for dinner. Catch up with that friend who always seems to say what you need to hear most. Look around and name everything you're thankful for. Treat yourself tenderly and see if it doesn't help your whole life feel a bit cozier.

No. 22 Taking Stock

One way to start being kinder to yourself is to take stock of the qualities you're thankful for. This is not a space to note things you'd like to improve or work on; this is for the good stuff that you already do well and feel good about.

What are the things you like about yourself?

....

....

....

What do you do well?

....

....

....

....

Which accomplishments are you proud of? These don't have to be awards or even big events. You can be proud for being a patient, gentle parent or for pouring love into your relationship and keeping it strong. You can be proud of the loving home you've created.

....

....

....

....

How do you think your loved ones would describe you?

What would they say you do well?

What would they say they like best about you?

Which of your traits makes you feel happiest? Most peaceful? Most confident?

What are you most thankful for about yourself?

What are you most thankful for about your life?

NO. 23 Letter to Your Past Self

our vintage brass
candlesticks were collected

Find some quiet time in your day and use this space to write a letter to Past You with everything she needs to hear. Speak to her with kindness. What do you want her to forgive herself for? Is there shame she's holding onto that she can release? What failures and mistakes can she stop blaming herself for so she can move forward in peace? How can she express her love for that past version of herself? What can you tell her that you know now, and how has that knowledge changed things for you? Take the time to write it all out, and then read it aloud to yourself. You—past, present, and future—deserve to hear it.

Dear Past Self,

NO. 24 Finding Everyday Joy

Prioritizing joy is a big part of a cozy lifestyle. No amount of money or pretty décor can make up for a life that isn't filled with joy. Joy is what takes a house from beautiful but cold to warm and cozy. It took me a while to figure that out.

Joy has a way of seeping into places. When we choose to prioritize joy and love and fun in our homes, that energy doesn't leave when times get difficult. It's still there, waiting to comfort us when we grieve, bolster us when we feel frustrated, and calm us when we get angry.

I think that for most of us, joy is found in so many simple things. I find joy at home more than anywhere else. It's in digging in the garden dirt, lying in the warm sunshine, listening to Cope laugh and splash in the bath, slipping between freshly washed sheets at the end of a long day, eating pasta by candlelight with my family, strolling back from the snowy barn toward the warm glow of light through the windows, walking our dogs hand in hand with Jose. Little moments of joy add up to the coziest life.

What brings you joy?

Suze Orman
THE COURAGE TO BE RICH
THE PRIZE
THE END of LOYALTY
Women After All
CRASHED
Martina Navratilova
Women After All
Never Leaves You
Stones into Schools
TEN, the Secret Radical
Condoleezza Rice
EXTRAORDINARY, ORDINARY PEOPLE
SUZE ORMAN • THE COURAGE TO BE RICH
Chicken Soup for the Soul
JUDITH KRANTZ
DAZZLE
RITZ & ESCOFFIER
LUKE BARR
LOVE
DAVE ISAY
THE HONEYMOON
DINITIA SMITH
COMEBACK CHURCHES
Ellen Feldman
THE GROWTH DELUSION
DAVID PILLING
Maxine Clair
October Suite

No. 25 Cozy Online

I'll be the first to admit that I spend way too much time on my phone—many of us do, right? I love that I can connect with people, share my business and my home through my blog, find inspiration, and shop for vintage finds. But sometimes, the Internet hurts more than it helps.

Have you ever found yourself mindlessly scrolling, seeing beautiful image after beautiful image, each more perfect and polished than the previous one, and thought to yourself, *I will never be that perfect,* or *My home will never be that nice*? The images we see are almost never the whole truth. They are an edited, carefully crafted bite of someone's life that is served up on social media as if it's the whole meal. It's *meant* to make you want something. If you are scrolling in a good head space, it may not be a problem; but if you aren't at your best, it can make you feel horrible, compel you to overspend, or simply waste a lot of time that keeps you from being present in your own life.

When I find that happening, I know it's time to make a change. I start with unfollowing accounts that are mentally draining and stay far away from online communities that feel toxic. I also stop reading comments so I'm not tempted into a comment war. Instead, I focus on the corners of the Internet that inspire me and make me feel positive and optimistic about my life and the world around me.

If that's not enough, I take a real break. I log out of my accounts or delete the apps for a while and go analog. I call or meet up with my friends and family for in-person conversations and play with Cope in the sunshine. I take walks in nature, work in my garden, and read actual books. Then, when I'm feeling cozier and more settled in my life, I can return to the Internet on healthier terms.

No. 26 Letter to Your Future Self

One of the best reasons to create a cozier life is so that Future You can feel empowered to flourish in new and exciting ways. Think about what you want for your future self and write her a letter. This can be personal, about your work or family, or even about how you'd like your cozy home to come together. How do you hope she is growing over the next five years? Ten years? What are your hopes and dreams and vision for your life moving forward?

Dear Future Self,

NO. 27 MARCH HOME MAINTENANCE CHECKLIST

Every year, I get very antsy by March. I'm *so* over the snow and ready for spring, but we usually still have some winter ahead of us here in Michigan. Since I can't spend as much time as I'd like outside, March is when I focus on spring cleaning indoors, putting away winter décor, and freshening up to usher in spring.

	MARCH HOME MAINTENANCE CHECKLIST					
	Check and/or replace batteries in your smoke detectors and carbon monoxide detectors. If any of these items are more than seven years old, it's time to replace them.					
	Inspect your roof for missing, loose, or damaged shingles from winter storms. Get any issues fixed before spring rains cause leaks!					
	Clean gutters and downspouts. Melting snow can lead to clogs.					
	Inspect the exterior of your chimney for any winter damage.					
	Rake up any leftover leaves from your lawn.					
	If you use weed killer, March is a good time to put down pre-emergent in beds to avoid weed growth. Check labels and ingredients to find a safe product for your family and pets.					
	Start prepping your outdoor spaces when the weather allows. If you live somewhere like Michigan where summer is shorter, you'll want to be ready to enjoy every possible moment of warm weather outside.					

	If you have central air-conditioning, schedule an HVAC spring tune-up. If you use window units, clean your unit based on the manufacturer's instructions and get it ready for summer use.					
	Begin indoor spring cleaning. Focus on deep-cleaning tasks like dusting blinds and fan blades, reversing the settings on your fans to counterclockwise to push down cool air, wiping down baseboards, polishing floors, deep-cleaning carpets, and cleaning light fixtures and upholstered pieces like sofas and chairs. I also recommend cleaning appliances like your refrigerator, dishwasher, oven, and range hood. Pro Tip: this doesn't have to be done all at once! I like to go room by room, and it usually takes me a few weeks.					
	Put away winter décor and pull out some favorite spring items for an instant mood lift!					
	Clean the garbage disposal.					
	Check your HVAC filters and change them as needed.					
	Vacuum your dryer's lint trap.					
	Check your water softener system.					
	Check the temperature on your water heater.					
	If you have pets, give them their monthly flea, tick, and heart guard medicines.					

No. 28 Knowing Your Paint Colors

A big part of knowing your home is knowing the colors on your walls, your wallpaper, and your trim and ceilings.

After spending months selecting the perfect shade of blue for your bedroom, you might think that you couldn't possibly forget the name of the color, but I promise it's more likely to happen than you think! Plus, you need to remember the finish as well. You do not want to touch up a satin wall with a semi-gloss paint. Even the nap on your roller can make a difference in how the wall looks.

This information is also super helpful when a wall gets dinged, scraped, or colored on with permanent marker. You can find the correct paint easily if you have some left, or you can get a test pot of the color you need.

I usually paint my walls white. I feel like white walls create a beautiful backdrop that recedes into the background and allows my antiques and décor to really pop. But I don't use the same shade of white in every room of my home. Different light sources, the direction a room faces, flooring colors, and furniture all affect the tone of white walls. I test large swatches in a room and look at them at different times of day and with different combinations of lamps and overhead lights to make sure I love *that* particular shade before making a choice. So even if you think you know the color you want, I highly recommend painting some swatches and making sure of your choice before you go all in and paint the whole room! It will save you a lot of time and money.

Turn to the Cozy Home Guide at the back of the book and use the marked pages to write down and track each paint color and finish in your home. The next time you're at the hardware store, grab the corresponding swatches and tape those in your journal for reference as well. You can also cut swatches of wallpaper for future color matching.

Cozy Tip

When touching up paint around your home, you may need to let a spot dry overnight before putting on a second coat. No need to wash your brush between painting sessions. Put the brush into a plastic bag and stash it in the freezer overnight. The next day, let it thaw, and you can get right back to painting. Just don't leave it in the freezer ***too*** long (more than two to three days) or the paint will dry out.

No. 29 Bucket Lists and Dreams

I talked a little bit about this in *Cozy White Cottage*, but it bears repeating: don't wait for your life to begin. We all tend to wait for the perfect moment to do big things like starting a family, opening a business, putting yourself out there—whatever it is for you. But there never will be a perfect moment because life isn't perfect. You will never feel fully ready.

Sometimes you just have to take a leap of faith. Will it go perfectly? Maybe not, but you'll be further along than when you started. Instead of waiting for perfection, work with what you have in the moment. Be flexible and let life surprise you. That temporary fix or step may just lead to something bigger and better than your original plan, but you won't know unless you stop waiting and start doing.

What are the things you would regret not having the chance to do?

....

....

....

For yourself?

....

....

....

For your partnership?

....

....

....

With your kids?

....

....

....

With your friends?

....

....

....

....

....

With extended family?

....

....

....

A trip you'd like to take?

....

....

....

Something you'd like to create?

....

....

....

Something you want to do in your home?

....

....

....

A new skill you'd like to learn? A degree you'd like to earn?

....

....

....

....

Even if you can't do everything right now, don't wait to do things that make you happy. Make a plan. Set a savings goal. Take baby steps. But get started now!

NO. 30 TAKE THE FIRST STEP

You laid out some hopes and dreams for your future self in the previous entry, but we don't want them to *stay* hopes and dreams. We want them to become reality—a part of your everyday life.

So pick one or two things from the past few pages. In the space below, write out all the steps it will take you to go from dreaming to planning to doing to finishing. Try to think through all the details: What do you need to get going? Who can you ask for help? What do you need to research or learn? How can you fit this into your schedule without getting overwhelmed? Be as specific as you can.

Good work! Look at everything you wrote above. You've started (and maybe even finished) writing out your plan. That's the first step—you are on your way!

No. 31 Cozy Self-Love List

When life feels extra tough or you find yourself feeling drained and maybe a little burnt out, it is absolutely okay (and, in fact, recommended) to treat yourself to something a little special. This doesn't have to be expensive or even cost anything at all. I'm talking about a little treat that would really help you feel cozy when you need it most. For me, it's usually something like a bouquet of flowers or a new plant for the house, a hot bath and a good nap, or a dinner out so I don't have to cook.

For you, it may be taking a whole day to read in front of the fire or lounge outdoors. It might be buying grocery store flowers when spring feels far away or a large, iced coffee when the summer sun feels too hot. Maybe it's getting the *really good* coffee for those dark winter mornings or a pumpkin-spiced latte to sip as the leaves change.

What is something extra cozy you could do for yourself the next time you feel a little blue?

....

....

....

....

....

....

....

....

....

Cozy Tip

One of the things that helps me the most when I'm feeling down is to pick one of these little indulgences and treat someone else—a friend, family member, neighbor, or even a stranger. Sharing cozy is an instant pick-me-up.

No. 32 Spread Cozy

I learned *cozy* as a kid from my grandmother, and it's been a lifelong goal of mine to be the same sort of warm, inviting, and caring woman she was. Sometimes that means welcoming others into my home, both digitally and in person. Other times it means going out into my community to bring the cozy to people who need it most: friends, family, and organizations that know how to reach those in need.

Are you great at organizing? Offer to

help a neighbor clean out and organize their garage. Do you love to cook? Take a meal to a friend who is struggling with something. We love our animals around here, so of course we think donating time or supplies to animal shelters is always a great option. Look around for other opportunities to spread your personal brand of *cozy*: bake cookies for your child's teacher, help an elderly neighbor with their yardwork or a ride to an appointment, drop off soup for that new mom at your church.

From personal experience, I've learned never to ask a friend or family member, "Is there anything I can do?" during a difficult time, but to instead just show up and do something. People will say no because they don't want to feel like a burden or because they are so overwhelmed that they don't even know what they need.

We all have something to give. Just keep your eyes open for opportunities to share your time, talents, and treasures with others.

What are some issues in the world or your community that you feel passionately about?

....

....

....

....

Which of your talents could you use to help others?

....

....

....

....

Who in your life could use some help or encouragement?

....

....

....

....

....

How could you use your gifts to help?

....

....

....

....

....

No. 33 April Home Maintenance Checklist

We occasionally get snow in April, but for the most part, the weather slowly but surely starts to inch toward spring. Of course, "April showers bring May flowers," so part of my April checklist is to prepare my garden and yard for early spring rains. And that always reminds me to get the rest of my house ready for spring too. I get excited to do those things because I know warm weather is coming and I want to be ready to enjoy every minute of it!

APRIL HOME MAINTENANCE CHECKLIST

	Clean and put away winter décor. Launder throw pillows and blankets, and pack them away with a sweet-smelling sachet so they'll be ready for you in the fall.					
	Change out slipcovers and launder the ones you've been using. I use brighter white slipcovers for the spring and summer and more neutral tones for the fall and winter.					
	Get out your spring décor and have fun freshening up your rooms.					
	Spring cleaning isn't just for the indoors. Wipe down and rinse your home's exterior, including windows, screens, and skylights. Reinstall screens if you removed them for the winter.					
	Walk around your home and look for any signs of damage or wear and tear that needs to be addressed: peeling paint, cracks in the foundation, dry rot to trim or siding, or signs of animal or insect damage. This is the time to get these issues handled.					

	Clean out fireplaces and close chimneys.						
	Clean and store snow-specific items like sleds, snow blowers, skis, and other winter items so they'll be ready to use next year.						
	Get out spring and summer equipment like garden shovels, hoes, and watering cans and toys. Clean off, tune up, and gas up your lawn mower, weeder, edger, and blower for summer lawn maintenance. You may need to have blades sharpened or repairs done, and it's best to do this before mowing season begins.						
	Check outdoor swings or playsets for winter damage. Get bikes and other outdoor toys ready for spring and summer.						
	Get started planting any new landscaping and also your summer garden.						
	Fertilize your lawn.						
	Prep and start your flower beds as the weather allows.						
	Clean the garbage disposal.						
	Check your HVAC filters and change them as needed.						
	Vacuum your dryer's lint trap.						
	Check your water softener system.						
	Check the temperature on your water heater.						
	If you have pets, give them their monthly flea, tick, and heart guard medicines.						

No. 34 Cozy Is Welcoming

Community is cozy. And it's crazy to me how many of us miss out on that life-giving connection because we're worried our homes aren't good enough. I know this struggle, and I'm here to tell you it's okay to invite people into your mess; they won't judge you a fraction as harshly as you are judging yourself. Your home doesn't have to be finished or perfectly clean to host—it just needs to be welcoming and loving.

It took me a little while to get over my own insecurities about my home to invite people in, but I am *so* glad I did. Here are my best tips if you are ready to stop stressing and start connecting in your own home.

- Give your home a quick clean before guests arrive but don't get carried away. Your friends know that you *live* in your home, and it's perfectly okay if it looks like it.
- Keep food simple and easy so you can enjoy talking to your guests. An artfully arranged cheeseboard, chips, and veggies with delicious dip options or plates of store-bought pastries all make wonderful appetizers and snacks.
- Make a drink station. Whip up a pitcher of something yummy and set it in an easy-to-access spot along with cups, mix-ins, and ice, and let your guests pour for themselves. In the spring and summer, I love a basil lemonade; in the fall, an apple cider. And in the winter, you can't go wrong with a hot cocoa bar!
- This isn't prom, so you don't need a theme and over-the-top decorations. A few flowering branches or blooms from your yard in pretty vases are quick and beautiful.
- Keep flow and seating in mind. Make sure you allow space for guests to move from room to room—and indoors and outdoors—as needed. Create small groupings of seats for more intimate conversations during bigger gatherings. Entertaining a smaller group? Create a circular seating option so everyone can get in on the fun!

When you see a beautifully styled room on my Instagram feed, what you don't see is the mess piled up just outside the frame—Cope's toys, Jose's tools, the dust and debris from our latest project.

No. 35 Cozy Gathering Ideas

Entertaining doesn't have to happen only around the holidays. We're big on family dinners, game nights, and just-because get-togethers, especially in warm weather. I know with the busy-ness of work, life, and kids, sometimes it's hard to generate the energy to plan something. Here's a list of a few of my favorite (and easy) reasons to plan a gathering:

- Game nights with friends. If you and your friends have kids, consider hiring a sitter to look after everyone while you spend time together.
- Big game days
- Movie nights
- Pool parties
- Dinners with colleagues or friends from church

In those cases, I don't feel a lot of pressure to decorate or try to make everything look perfect. Beautiful and cozy, yes. Perfect, no. And a few fun touches—think favorite childhood snacks served at game night, or freshly popped popcorn and boxes of candy for movie night, or color-coordinated pool floats and pitchers of strawberry lemonade while splashing in the pool—give even last-minute hangouts a fun, festive feel.

Entertaining is *always* about connection over perfection. A few thoughtful touches go a long way. What's more important is making sure your guests feel comfortable, welcome, and cozy. Prioritize *those* things, and I promise every gathering will be a success.

Now, write your idea list and try to get something on the calendar!

No. 36 Cozy Hosting

Okay, I've shared all my entertaining secrets, so now it's up to you to figure out how to invite others into your home, despite how finished (or not) it is, in a way that works for you and your family.

The best way to get started is to set some goals and start working toward them. Use the space below to think through options and make plans to start hosting more often.

Start small.

Do you have a favorite holiday?

Why is it your favorite? What about it makes you so happy?

How can you share that with others in your home?

Could you offer to host family or friends for that holiday?

Who are the people in your life you'd feel most excited/least stressed to invite over for some fun?

....

....

....

....

Is there an occasion coming up that would work for hosting? A holiday, sports game, or birthday?

....

....

How much time do you have to prepare?

....

....

....

Realistically, what would you need to do to prepare for hosting? (No, I'm not talking about big house projects that need to be completed!)

....

....

What would you like to serve for food and drinks?

....

....

What are a few décor choices that would be easy but make a big impact?

....

....

....

No. 37 Holiday Hosting

I love having the chance to lean into whatever holiday it happens to be and finding new ways to make it feel special. This has been especially important to me since Cope joined the family.

I grew up with a wealth of family traditions, and carrying some of those forward, as well as making new ones, is extremely important to me. I love the idea of routinely baking a dish or hosting an annual party or putting up decorations in a special way to make memories each year—something everyone can look forward to and cherish. Since becoming Copeland's mama, I look forward to each holiday season like I'm a kid again myself. As I watch the pure joy on his face when he sees the Christmas tree or spots the front porch decked with pumpkins for fall or runs downstairs to find his Easter baskets, it truly makes each holiday brand new for me and Jose.

Here are a few tips that may help you anticipate and solve the more common tricky issues that come with holiday hosting:

- Confirm head count for each adult guest in advance.
- If your family is close and rarely fights, let people sit wherever they want. If, on the other hand, friendly discussions tend to turn into less-friendly quarrels at family gatherings, plan seating ahead of time with place cards that will direct everyone to their assigned seat and can easily be part of your décor for an extra-festive feel.
- If the whole group doesn't fit around one big table, you'll want to create several small tables. Seat people near others they enjoy spending time with or who are close together in age

and have common interests. A children's table is great for older kids, but you'll want to seat toddlers with their parents. Set up your tables one to two days in advance so you don't have to stress about it the day of.

- Set up a buffet area for serving food so that you aren't passing items around the table all night. A kitchen island, kitchen table, or even card tables work well for this. If I don't need the same space for food prep, I set out each serving dish with accompanying spoons, forks, or ladles the day before so I know exactly where to put things when it's go-time.
- Delegate. Hosting is a big job, and you can ask others to bring side dishes, drinks, appetizers, or desserts—especially things that are served cold or room temperature.
- Think through details that make guests feel comfortable and cozy. Are the bathrooms stocked with plenty of towels, toilet paper, and deodorizing spray? Are there enough chairs for everyone to sit and visit? Enough tables and ledges for people to set down drinks? Do you have enough ice on hand? Do you have a playlist ready for background ambience? Does your home get hot easily? If so, get fans going or turn on the AC a couple of hours before guests arrive. Is your home always drafty and chilly? Turn up the heat or get a fire going in the fireplace before everyone comes in.
- Keep décor simple but impactful. On Thanksgiving, we spend most of our time around the table, so I focus on pretty place settings. At Christmas, we all sit around the tree, so I focus my efforts on a beautiful tree and cozy pillows and blankets for lounging. At Easter, I fill bowls and vases with dyed eggs to add beautiful color.
- Take lots of pictures or designate someone to be the event photographer. Hosting will keep you busy, and later you'll be glad to see photos of everyone enjoying your home and hard work.

NO. 38 May Home Maintenance Checklist

May is the month when spring really arrives in Michigan. After a long winter and being stuck inside, you'll find me outside with my hands in the dirt even on the chilliest May days! It's the perfect time to get your yard, garden, pool, and porches ready for the summer fun ahead.

MAY HOME MAINTENANCE CHECKLIST						
	Repair or replace caulking and weather stripping around windows, doors, and mechanicals.					
	Remove insulation from outdoor faucets and check water flow. Check hoses and sprinklers to make sure they are in good working order and aren't damaged.					
	If you have an irrigation system, inspect it and make repairs before setting its spring and summer schedule.					
	Plant annuals and perennials to brighten up your curb appeal. While you're at it, remove and compost any plants that didn't make it through the winter.					
	Add mulch to your flower and garden beds to prevent weeds, keep soil temperature and moisture levels consistent, and help your awakening plants grow.					
	Continue to fertilize your lawn, focusing on any bare spots that didn't take as well last month. Or, if prior fertilization didn't yield results, you may want to sod those areas.					

	Deadhead flowers and bushes as needed and dig up weeds weekly. Water your plants often to protect them from the heat.					
	Clean your grill so it's ready for barbecue season.					
	If you have a generator, make sure it's in good working order in the case of brownouts as the weather heats up.					
	Give your porches, patios, and other outdoor living spaces a good scrub.					
	Unpack your outdoor cushions and pillows, and style your outdoor living spaces for warm days and longer evenings spent outside.					
	Clean the garbage disposal.					
	Check your HVAC filters and change them as needed.					
	Vacuum your dryer's lint trap.					
	Check your water softener system.					
	Check the temperature on your water heater.					
	If you have pets, give them their monthly flea, tick, and heart guard medicines.					

No. 39 Growing Things

I feel most alive and happy when I'm around plants, both indoors and outdoors. There is something about connecting with nature on any level that feeds my soul. From growing seeds to tending fruiting plants or coaxing along lovely little rosemary topiaries, it all calls to me. I wouldn't say I have a green thumb, exactly—I've had plenty of garden and landscaping fails over the years—but I'd certainly say it's green-ish and getting greener all the time. Some people certainly have natural talent when it comes to growing things, but anyone can learn to garden and can improve their skills with a little research and hands-on experience.

When we started gardening, I had very little knowledge about it, but I knew that I loved plants, and I knew that I wanted them in and around my home. It felt like a natural extension of growing and improving our home little by little, and I really *wanted* to learn. I think that part is key.

I've learned that if you force yourself to grow something that never bears fruit for you or your family (pun intended), you'll never truly enjoy the process. If you want to learn to feed your family by growing some of your own fruits and vegetables, you can. If you want to fill your yard with flowers or trees and bushes, you can. Yes, you will need to buy a few things to get started, but the biggest investment will be your own time and energy.

If you feel hesitant and unsure of where to start, I've been there. Start small and start in places in or outside your home where you already enjoy spending time. Over the next several days, I'm going to share my tips and the things I've learned about growing things. I hope they inspire you to go out and get your hands dirty and that you find it as therapeutic as I always do!

Now I can't imagine *not* having a garden or tending our plants and trees each spring, summer, and fall. We have

some form of living greenery around our home all year long. Growing things has become part of our rhythm here on White Cottage Farm, and the process has taught me so much, both practically and spiritually, about preparation, patience, nurturing, growth, problem solving, and abundance. We were created to live in harmony with the seasons, and nothing drives that home quite like a garden.

Whether you are a seasoned gardener or a total newbie, if you feel that "pull" to get your hands into the dirt and create something for yourself and your family, I highly encourage you to start now. No matter the season, there is something you can do to get started.

No. 40 Preparing for Cozy Gardens

Landscaping has a big impact on the curb appeal of your home but isn't always super easy to figure out, especially if you don't have lots of experience with plants. Still, it's worth the research because the right landscaping will make your home so much happier and cozier. The same is true for gardens.

Before you pick what types of plants you want, it's good to know what types of plants will suit your home. Here are my tips to start creating your personalized garden and landscaping plan.

- Walk around your home once an hour on a nice sunny day. Make a basic sketch of your home and where plants will go, and note how much sun each of those areas gets every hour: full sun, partial sun, partial shade,

or full shade. You'll need this information to know where to put garden beds and which plants to select for your landscaping.

- Identify your growing zone and stick to it when planning and purchasing.
- Think through potential garden areas for flowers, herbs, or vegetables that will be convenient for you and will get the necessary amounts of sun or shade.
- Measure the areas where you need to put plants. The baby plants you install will get bigger, and you'll want to plant with the recommended mature size and dimensions in mind. Make sure you leave a little space around the plant: remember, you need to think about how big the mature plant will be and how close it will be to the side of your house (you don't want problems with drainage, bugs, or roots pushing against your foundation!). This is also helpful when it's time to prune your plant and you've left yourself space to work.
- Research the best times of year to plant. Trees often should be planted in the fall, while other plants do best in the spring. Various fruits and vegetables can be planted at different times from spring through fall. Look up frost times for your area to help you plan.
- Landscaping should consist mainly of shrubbery and perennial plants that look nice year-round. You can always add a few annuals each season to keep things fresh.

Cozy Tip

Once you know what plants you need and where you want to put them, continue to map out a plan for both your time and budget. In addition to plants, you may also need good soil, manure, peat moss, other soil amendments, and mulch.

No. 41 The Selection Process

Make a list of plants you and your family would enjoy and benefit from. For those cooks out there, herb gardens, tomatoes, and lettuce are all easy and popular starters. For landscapers, well-appointed trees and shrubs can be game-changers for curb appeal (and the environment!). And for decorative gardeners, make a short list of your favorite ornamental plants and flowers.

Fruits and Vegetables

....

....

....

Perennial Flowers

....

....

....

Trees and Shrubs

....

....

....

Annual Flowers

....

....

....

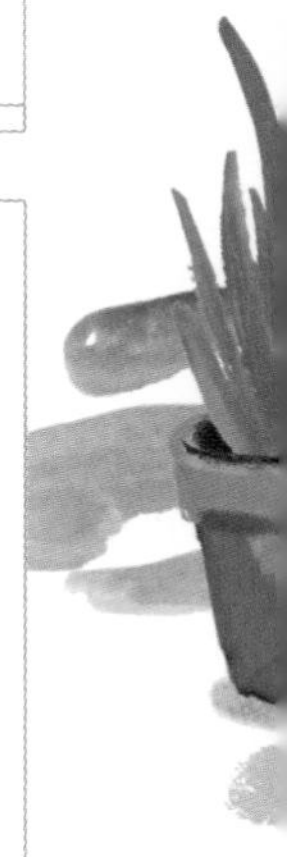

Cozy Tip

Walk around your neighborhood and other neighborhoods in your area. If you have an iPhone, take a photo and select the little "i" with the stars next to it. Guess what? Your phone can identify the plant! There are countless plant identifier apps out there that will give you great results, such as Seek by iNaturalist, PlantIn, and PictureThis. If a plant grows well for your neighbors, chances are it will work in your yard too.

A FEW OF MY FAVORITES:

Trees and Shrubs:

- Pear Trees
- Boxwood Shrubs
- Yew Shrub

Perennial flowers:

- Hydrangea (especially the ***arborescens*** and ***paniculata*** varieties—the names we know them by locally are Limelight, Annabelle, and Incrediball)
- Lavender

No. 42 Get Growing

Now that you know what your location is suited for, start small and *grow* your passion—something you are excited to nourish and coax along, whether that means new or updated landscaping, vegetables, fruit, herbs, or flowers. When you are just starting, your goal should simply be to enjoy the gardening process. Do a little self-reflection and determine where and what your gardening needs and wishes are.

- Based on the sketch you made, your wish list, and your neighborhood favorites, make a basic plan for which plants you'd like to put where and how many you might need

based on your measurements. I always try to give myself a few options since I won't know what will be available until I begin shopping.

- I recommend starting at a local nursery rather than a big box store simply because the people who work there are so knowledgeable and can share all sorts of information.
- When you find a plant you like, buy one and bring it home. Set it where you would like to plant it to make sure it looks great with the other neighboring plants, as well as the color of your home.
- Once you've found the right things, get them planted in good soil, top with mulch, and give them plenty of water so they can grow and last for many years.

For Landscaping

Your plan should consider how large your plants will grow and the colors they'll become throughout the year. If you're planting double rows, you'll want taller plants in the back and shorter options in the front. I suggest mixing evergreens with more colorful shrubs. I also suggest making sure you have a mix of plants that show color in different seasons.

For Fruit and Vegetable Gardening

I find it helpful to have my beds ready before I purchase plants. That way my new little plants can go straight into good soil and not have to stay in their pots or trays longer than necessary. If a current bed or plot doesn't already exist, consider getting them ready before you make purchases.

No. 43 Growing Flowers

How wonderful would it be to have a fresh supply of flowers during spring, summer, and fall that you can enjoy, both outdoors and in? Growing beautiful flowers is easier than most people think. I know that sounds overly simple, but that's because it *is* simple. When I first started, gardening felt intimidating to me because there seemed to be *so many rules*. But once I got started, I realized that there are only four hard-and-fast rules:

1. Choose flowers that grow well in your zone.
2. Make sure your flowerbeds get the suggested amount of sunlight.
3. Fill your beds with good soil. Check with local greenhouses that have great dirt for pots and beds. Soil from local nurseries is typically perfect for your area.
4. Water your flowers regularly.

For beginners, I suggest planting a mix of easy-to-grow flowers with a few more delicate varieties. Look for something with colors that you love, something that attracts pollinators, and something that smells beautiful to you. That way you'll have something to cut and bring into your home, something for the butterflies and bees, and something that fills the air with the smell of spring. I can just smell my peonies as I think about it! Here are some ideas:

- If your goal is a colorful garden, try zinnias, ranunculus, or dahlias.
- For the butterflies and bees, plant pansies, snapdragons, and catmint.
- If your goal is a heady, floral scent in your garden, plant lavender, gardenias, or lilacs.
- If you like the look of a cottage garden, plant Queen Anne's lace, violets, and hydrangeas.

Cozy Tip

There are a few things you can do to make your bouquets last longer so you can enjoy them for weeks instead of a few days. Here are the ones I like best.

- Cut stems on an angle.
- Change the water every few days.
- Clear out leaves under the water line.
- There are a lot of folk remedies for keeping your flowers going strong, like adding aspirin, Sprite, or pennies to the water. Do a little research for tips specific to the flowers you are using and give these tricks a try.

NO. 44

A Kitchen Garden

There is something so confidence-boosting about growing food for your family to eat. It is such a sense of accomplishment to pull the first vegetable or herb off the plant and get to eat it with your people. Growing up, my parents always grew a few tomato plants on our back deck. They never grew anything else, but it was still a kitchen garden. A kitchen garden is just a spot—big or small—where you grow some food. It's accessible, easy to grow, and a great way to feel more connected to what you eat.

Those tomatoes my parents grew inspired me. Since Jose and I work from home, we have more time and energy for a garden, but ours still isn't huge. We grow tomatoes, cucumbers, radishes, squash, pumpkins, and herbs.

My best tip for a kitchen garden is to be honest with yourself. Which vegetables and herbs do you eat regularly? How much gardening and tending do you have time for? You want to grow your garden to work *with* your lifestyle. Grow what you love—not what you think you *should*.

A FEW QUESTIONS TO ASK YOURSELF:

Is your yard rocky or clay-based? If so, you may need raised beds.

Do you get a lot of wildlife visitors? You may need a fence to protect your plants.

Is your yard flat or hilly? Pumpkins and squash grow well on hills, but other plants do best on flat land.

Our Favorite Easy-to-Grow Options

- Climbing beans
- Cucumbers
- Herbs
- Lettuce
- Pumpkins
- Squash
- Strawberry
- Sweet Peas
- Tomatoes (we like Carolina Gold)

No. 45 Eating Your Harvest

Having a garden is literal farm-to-table eating. Since we started growing a garden, I've learned to eat more seasonally. As things become ripe, we eat them, preserve them, or pass them on to others. Cope and I start most summer mornings in the garden, watering, weeding, and harvesting what's ripe and ready. That gives me time to plan how to use my bounty at lunch and dinner each day. Tending a garden is a great education for little ones, and it makes my heart happy to see how much Cope enjoys tending plants alongside his dad and me.

There have been times when we got too busy and let our cilantro go to seed or veggies rot on the vine. It's not a good feeling. But it taught us to keep an eye on our garden and how to anticipate when things will be ripe so we can plan to use those items while they are at the peak of freshness. I often give our produce away when we have too much. But if you like to cook and preserve your own food, a garden is a great way to get started.

We eat a lot of summer salads since they are a great way to incorporate delicious homegrown veggies into each meal. Other ways to use summer produce are vegetable lasagnas, soups, stir fries, and trays of roasted vegetables to go with whatever Jose throws on the grill. I also make my own salsa, tomato sauce, and tomato soup when my tomatoes get ripe. While I don't jar or can things, I like to freeze vegetables and fruits that are freezer-friendly so I can pull them out in the dead of winter for a bright taste of summer. I clean, dry, and prep each item so it's ready for use and then scatter everything on big baking sheets that I place in the freezer for a few hours. Then I transfer the frozen produce into Ziploc bags, careful to get out as much air as possible to prevent freezer burn. The bags go back in the freezer and can stay there for about six months, ready to be used all winter long.

No. 46 My Favorite Gardening Tools

To start your gardening journey, make do with what you already have. If you try gardening and realize it's not for you, this will be easier to admit if you haven't spent hundreds of dollars on equipment. The items I've listed below are things Jose and I have added to our shed over the years. Take your time and buy only what *you* need. If you aren't sure, many hardware stores rent electric tools, so you can try them before you buy them. Alternately, ask your family or neighbors if they have tools you can borrow.

I personally choose tools with a classic, vintage look that fit with my cozy cottage style. This is partially because I like to look at beautiful things, but also because my gardening tools get a lot of use and I like to have them within easy reach as they hang in my greenhouse or shed, where they double as décor.

Here are my favorites:

- A sturdy spaded shovel with a nice long handle: I use this for digging out big rocks or roots, or when I need to shovel lots of mulch.
- A beautiful, lightweight watering can: Cope loves to help water our plants, and these are great for hard-to-reach plants and pots.
- A long, sturdy garden hose: I use my hoses a lot for everything from watering plants, to cleaning

off footpaths and patios, to filling water dishes for animals.

- A good quality garden hose reel.
- Action hoe: This nifty little tool will allow you to get under the root of weeds to pull them out without having to crouch down for hours.
- Garden shears: I suggest getting several different sizes and varieties. We use them for almost everything in the garden—pruning, deadheading, cutting back weeds, and snipping ripe vegetables from the vine.
- Auger: This makes it much easier to plant seeds and is especially useful when you have hard or clay soil that is tough to dig into.
- Tote or wagon: We use a little wagon or handy totes for carting our tools, plants, and seedlings to wherever we are going to plant them.
- Seed starter trays: These are wonderful little inventions for starting seeds and getting them ready for real planting.
- Gardening gloves: These protect your hands and make gardening much more pleasant.
- Wheelbarrow: We use ours to haul everything from rocks, to mulch, to compost, to leaves.
- Raised garden beds: If you have rocky or clay-logged soil, raised beds will be a huge help to you.
- Cultivator: A cultivator is used to churn up dirt for tilling. For smaller gardens, a hand-cranked one would work well; for a larger area, I recommend an electric one.
- Rake: A lightweight, easy-to-hold rake makes dealing with fall leaves far easier.
- Garden hoe: This is a huge help to prepare the ground for planting and to cover seeds.
- Mini-chainsaw: A handheld, battery-powered chainsaw is so much easier to use than a full-sized chainsaw, but they have plenty of power to cut through branches and roots.
- Trenching shovel: This is a long, skinny version of a regular spade. We use it for transplanting plants and general planting. Its size and shape cuts faster into the ground.
- Post-hole digger: This is a must if you need to dig holes big enough to plant trees and large bushes.

NO. 47 THE GIFT OF A GARDEN

The better we've gotten at gardening, the bigger our bounty has become. That's a wonderful thing, but it also can be a challenge because, even if you love tomatoes, there are only so many you can eat before you need a break! We give lots of our produce away to friends and family, and it feels so special to give loved ones something you grew yourself.

During the past few years, we decided to be more intentional about blessing others with our garden. We began to plant vegetables and herbs that we don't eat ourselves but that others in our lives love. Dropping off a basket of fresh produce we grew ourselves each week has been such a fun way to show our people how much they mean to us.

If you love gardening but can't keep up with how much you grow, look around for people you can bless with your bounty. Friends, family, neighbors, and your local food bank or shelter could all benefit from your hard work. If you want to get a little creative, whip up some jars of homemade salsa or pasta sauce, or bake a pie with fruit you grew yourself. Tie them with ribbon and tags and leave them as gifts to say thank you to first responders in your community, for librarians at your local library, or for anyone you think could use a treat. I also find that seeds or cuttings from my plants alongside small pots, a pretty shovel, and a nice set of gardening gloves make the perfect gift for Teacher Appreciation Week each March. The bigger your garden grows, the more chances you have to share its blessings and grow your community as you do!

GATE

No. 48 June Home Maintenance Checklist

We basically live outdoors during the summer, so it's no surprise that my June list consists of almost entirely outdoor chores. Somehow, doing work out in the sunshine doesn't feel as much like work. I do my best to get all the outdoor things done early in the month so I can spend the rest of the summer enjoying my outdoor spaces with Cope and Jose and hosting barbecues and pool parties with our friends and family.

JUNE HOME MAINTENANCE CHECKLIST						
	Clean your deck, porch, or patio and check for any damage. Apply a fresh coat of stain or sealant if needed.					
	If you have a pool, open it for the summer. Remove your cover, fill to the appropriate water level, check all equipment to make sure it's working properly, stock up on pool chemicals and other supplies, and get your pool ready to use. This is also a good time to schedule maintenance if you use a pool service. If you care for the pool yourself, set a schedule for maintenance and stick to it.					
	Check outdoor drainage. Areas that stay boggy or fill with stagnant water are signs you may need a more comprehensive drainage solution. This is especially important if water is accumulating around your foundation or leaking into your crawl space or basement.					
	Check and repair any fences on your property. Paint, stain, or seal if needed. Oil hinges and locks on gates.					

	Check your driveway. Pressure-wash as needed, fill cracks, and every few years, seal your driveway to keep it in good condition. If you have a gravel driveway, check your gravel levels and infill if needed.					
	Deadhead flowers and bushes as needed and dig up weeds weekly. Water your plants often to protect them from the heat.					
	Schedule annual pest control services.					
	Clean the garbage disposal.					
	Check your HVAC filters and change them as needed.					
	Vacuum your dryer's lint trap.					
	Check your water softener system.					
	Check the temperature on your water heater.					
	If you have pets, give them their monthly flea, tick, and heart guard medicines.					

No. 49
Cozy at the Table

When life gets busy and we don't have time for meals with our people, we lose out on that cozy connection point. Sitting together, chatting, and eating nourishing food fills us up in both body and soul. You don't have to be an award-winning chef to pull together meals that your family will love. In fact, simple is often better. The important part is the act of eating together.

I look forward all day to dinner with Jose and Cope. It's such a great time to come together, slow down enough to eat at an actual table, and talk about our days, what we are grateful for, and to make each other laugh a little. If dinner isn't doable because of busy schedules, you can always make breakfast your family's cozy meal. Starting the day together with intention is especially wonderful on winter mornings, when you can carry that cozy warmth with you all day long.

If you haven't had time for family meals lately or just need some new things to talk about, here are some fun questions to get everyone talking and laughing together:

- What was the best thing that happened to you today? What was the most challenging?
- How were you kind to someone today?
- How was someone kind to you?
- If you could eat only one meal for the rest of your life, what would it be?
- Name three things you like most about each member of the family.
- If you could go on vacation anywhere in the world, where would you choose and why?
- Name one family rule you'd like to see disappear.
- Name one family rule you'd like us to add.
- If you could trade places with a character in a book, which character would you choose?

- If you could create a new national holiday, what would it be?
- If you could create a new rule at school, what would you choose?
- Which animal do you think everyone in the family would be? Why?
- What's the best day you've ever had? Why?

No. 50 Creating Sustainable Health

My health journey started toward the end of 2020. Nothing huge happened that inspired me to make changes. I was just *really, really, really* uncomfortable. I knew I'd gained weight, but I was shocked when I realized it was more than forty pounds. I was always tired, and even bending down to tie my shoes was difficult. I felt older than I should, and I knew that my life would be better if I *felt* better.

I had become disconnected from my body. I think years of miscarriages and infertility had complicated my relationship with myself, and I recognized that I needed to change the way I treated my body to heal that relationship.

At the beginning, I just wanted to lose a little

weight and have more energy for keeping up with Cope. So, I joined a gym and started working out regularly. That helped me feel a little better, but I really didn't see much of a change. That's when I realized that just walking on the treadmill every week wasn't going to cut it. If I wanted to really improve my health, then I had to be willing to change my lifestyle. I needed to challenge the patterns I'd fallen into and try new things.

I started doing light weightlifting in addition to walking. I felt very intimidated walking into that section of the gym and picking up a two-pound weight, but over time it felt less uncomfortable. Now lifting weights is an important part of my routine, and I miss it when I have to take a few days off. Turns out, you don't have to sweat every day in the gym to get your body moving. I found a gentler pace that worked for me, and it felt so much better.

What really surprised me was that treating my body more tenderly has helped me take better care of *all* of me. I'm gentler with my feelings and emotions. I'm kinder to myself when I make mistakes, and I've stopped setting unreachable expectations for myself. Making my body healthier has made *all* of me healthier. It hasn't been easy, but I am so grateful for everything I've learned about myself and grateful that I've found a way of living and caring for myself that is healthy, sustainable, and makes me feel my best.

Over the next several days, we're going to talk more about food, fitness, and our overall health.

Cozy Tip

Do you have a favorite TV show? Do you love audiobooks or podcasts? Listening to or watching something I love can be extra motivating for indoor workouts.

No. 51 Your Fitness Journey

I love sharing my journey, but when I do, I know yours might look a little different than mine. And that's okay! What I know is that every body needs to move.

Personally, I really need accountability and a routine. Jose and I go to the gym a couple of times a week, and we work out at home on the off days. I'll share my favorite ways to move and exercise, and I hope to help you discover yours. You'll be amazed how getting into a routine you love feels like wonderful, cozy self-care.

I love weightlifting and barre movements. I love simple and slow routines. Find what you really enjoy and what works for your body.

Now, let's discover how you might love to move:

Cozy Tip

I love going to the gym, but I realize that's not ideal for everyone. And having the space at home to carve out a room dedicated to fitness is not always possible. However, when home is your favorite or easiest place to exercise, I've found that creating a cozy corner makes it so much more inviting. If you have a bike or treadmill, consider adding some plants and inspirational art nearby. Find a cute basket or bin to hold your yoga mat and weights. Create your own personal destination to exercise and love your body well.

What are your favorite ways to exercise? Think of things you can do anywhere, year-round, as well as things that are seasonal.

What do you absolutely hate doing?

Where do you love to exercise? At home, outdoors, the gym, or somewhere else?

Is it possible for you to exercise in a way you love every day? Five days a week? If not, what needs to change?

Write out your ideal exercise routine.

No. 52 A Health Journey That Works for You

It was around the time I started exercising that I also started seeing a doctor, and I realized then that my diet had to change. I had joined the gym so I could eat whatever I wanted, but the more I invested in my body, the more I realized that all the junk food I was eating wasn't serving me well. I also realized that so much of my relationship with food had everything to do with my feelings and little to do with how hungry I actually was. I started going to therapy and seeing a chiropractor, and I overhauled *how* and *what* I ate.

I had some really bad habits that were sabotaging my energy

levels. I ate until I was uncomfortably full at every meal, and I chose processed foods that were quite inflammatory to my body. I had been drinking at least two liters of Cherry Coke every day. I craved that caffeine and sugar and really leaned on that. I was so used to drinking it that I didn't notice how much worse I felt shortly after finishing each glass. The worse I felt, the more I drank, and the more I drank, the worse I felt. I stopped drinking soda, and within a week, I felt so much better that I realized I no longer wanted it anymore. I also cut way back on sugar and focused on eating whole, anti-inflammatory foods instead of more processed options.

However, I never went on a true "diet." Diets don't work for me. If you tell me something is off-limits, I just want it more! Instead, I focused on my relationship with food and how different foods make me feel. I still eat pizza and tacos (because they are delicious), but I started paying attention to my body and noticing when I was actually full. I used to feel like I had to eat as much as possible at each meal, but I've learned to stop eating when I'm full, trusting there will be plenty left for me to eat if I'm hungry later. I've also paid close attention to which foods make me feel good and fill me with energy, and which foods make me feel tired and slow and grumpy. I now eat far less of the foods that make me feel bad.

There's a reason I call this a "health journey" instead of a diet. It's not one-size-fits-all. Each of our bodies is unique, and we all have different factors that contribute to how we feel. What works well for me might not work as well for you. If you don't feel your best and want to get to a healthier place where you feel better, get to know your own body. Pay attention to how you feel when you eat different foods and how you feel when you do different exercises. Pay attention to your feelings around food. Ask for help if you need it, and if a doctor doesn't feel like a partner, find a different one. Stop listening to everyone else and start paying attention to how *your body* feels and what *you* need. It's worth doing the work to create a lifestyle that makes you feel your best.

No. 53 Nourishing Food, Nourished Bodies

What you choose to eat is personal. You will never find me online talking about a popular diet or a new trend. That sort of thing has never worked for me. But I believe that what we choose to eat has a profound effect on how we feel.

When I was younger, I tried a lot of diets that helped me lose weight but made me feel awful. When I set out to change my lifestyle, that included the way I ate. It wasn't because I was trying to slim down—it was because I wanted to have more energy, to feel less tired and rundown, and I wanted to feel full and satisfied after I ate without feeling bloated and tired. I wanted to feel like the very best version of myself, the version of me that felt good enough to do all the things I wanted at work, at home, with Jose, and with my wild child Cope.

So I started making changes—slowly cutting out junk food and sodas and then made changes more quickly as I realized how much better I felt. These days I stick to the foods that really nourish my body and help me feel energetic and happy. I've found that not only do these foods help my body, but they help my mood too.

Basically, I stick to whole foods that are in season and minimally processed, and I stay away from most sugar. My younger self would think that sounded horrible and so limiting, but it really isn't. Instead of drive-thru burgers and fries, we grill our own burgers and make homemade fries in the air-fryer. Instead of buying premade salad dressings filled with sugar and preservatives to keep them shelf stable, I make my own in minutes that taste every bit as delicious over fresh vegetables straight from my kitchen garden. Instead of a can of chicken noodle soup, I make a big batch of my own from scratch, and freeze individual portions for a rainy day. I still like and eat the same things. I just choose less processed, healthier versions. It's more work, but I feel so much better that it really is worth it *for me*.

In the process of making these changes, I focused on how I felt after each meal, keeping track of which foods made me feel great and which didn't. What makes me feel tired and bloated may not bother you at all—I'm not here to yuck anyone's yum—but I do want to encourage you that if you don't feel your best, changing your diet can be a really impactful tool to help you feel better. Take notes after each meal about how you feel and try making some tweaks that work with your lifestyle. You may be surprised about how much better you feel after making just a few changes.

We all deserve to feel our best. I hope you can find the food lifestyle that helps you get there like I did.

No. 54 Finding the Foods That Love You

I'm amazed how writing things down can help me sort through things and work out a plan. You may not be ready to start a daily food journal, but I'd love to help you get started thinking through foods you love that are good for you, along with some foods you love that you may need to cut down on or replace.

For example, I mentioned I loved Cherry Coke, but it made me feel terrible. I also loved ice cream and sugary snacks. And you know what? I can totally have them on occasion and still feel good. But I needed to replace the sugary drinks with water. Let's work through some things to help you with your food journey:

What foods and beverages do you love to consume daily or weekly but make you concerned that you're not serving your body?

....

....

....

What are foods and beverages you love that you're confident are good for you?

....

....

Are there certain foods that make you feel bloated, tired, or sluggish? Anything that seems to follow with a headache?

....

....

What was the last meal you ate that made you feel great—energetic and satisfied but not overly full?

....

....

....

....

If time, money, and ability weren't issues, what would your meals look like?

....

....

....

....

Some changes I could make this week are:

....

....

....

....

MY FAVORITE FEEL-GOOD SNACKS:

1. Peanut butter protein apple dip
2. Cut-up veggies with dips or hummus
3. Chips with black bean dip
4. Popcorn
5. Sugar-free dark chocolate chips with nuts

NO. 55 MEAL PLANNING

Meal planning can be a useful tool that helps you put cozy, nourishing meals on the table for your family each week. But I know it can feel intimidating! That's a lot of planning and coordinating, and if it's not done well, you can end up with a lot of strange ingredients in your fridge and pantry that you throw out.

I've figured out how to meal plan for my family, and it has made a huge difference in my ability to stick to foods that work best for me and keep us from wasting groceries. It's easier than you think once you do a little organization. Set aside a two- to three-hour period one afternoon to set yourself up, and I promise, you'll save yourself hours and hours each week. Ready to get started?

1. Gather all of your recipes and no-recipe recipes (think no-brainers that you know how to make by heart, like a sandwich or stir-fry). These should be meals that you know everyone loves. I find it helpful to print out my recipes or make a copy of the cookbook page. For no-recipe recipes, I just write down the basics.
2. Organize the recipes by season. Then go season by season, and group together recipes with overlapping ingredients. Use sticky notes or paper clips to flag recipes that can be made in the Instant Pot or Crockpot. Using another color, do the same for recipes that freeze well, like casseroles.
3. Look at your schedule for most weeks and estimate how much time you have for cooking each day. Then write out a little guide. (See my example below!) Is there a day you have a late soccer practice? Plan an Instant Pot meal for that day or plan to eat leftovers. A day when you're done with work early and have no plans? That's the perfect night to make a more involved meal.

4. Finally, put together a few meal plans using your favorite recipes that fit the season. I have found that six meal plans is a great number to keep our family from getting bored (we're never eating the same thing that frequently). I also write a grocery list for each meal plan.
5. Each week, I choose one of my pre-made meal plans. I compare the grocery list to what I already have on hand and then get the rest from the store. I spend a few hours (usually on Sunday afternoon) cleaning and chopping vegetables, pre-cooking rice, and making sauces or salad dressing I'll need for the week ahead. This allows me to make recipes faster each evening, giving me more time to spend with Jose and Cope.

Sample Meal Plan

Sunday: (1 hour)
Roast chicken with mashed potatoes and dill butter carrots

Monday: (30 minutes)
Grain bowls using chicken and carrot leftovers from Sunday with rice, salad greens, and turmeric tahini sauce

Tuesday: (20 minutes)
No-recipe stir-fry

Wednesday: (10 minutes)
Instant Pot soup

Thursday: (45 minutes)
Chicken and broccoli casserole (make two and freeze one for the future)

Friday: (1 hour)
Personal pizzas using frozen pizza dough

Saturday: (usually busy)
No-recipe pasta with a garden salad and garlic bread

NO. 56 LOVELY LEFTOVERS

Is it just me, or does feeling prepared for your day make it feel less hectic and decidedly cozier? Enter: lovely leftovers. Sometimes leftovers get a bad rap, but they don't have to be gross or boring. In fact, there are lots of ways to repurpose leftovers for meals that feel fresh and save you so much time. Plus, utilizing leftovers makes it easier to eat at home and saves you loads of money. I think of them less as "leftovers" and more as "pre-prepped ingredients thoughtfully handled by my past self."

Here are some of my favorites:

- Turn roast chicken leftovers into sheet pan chicken nachos or chicken noodle soup, or pair with rice and greens in a grain bowl.
- Cook a double batch of ground beef. Use half for Taco Tuesday and save the rest for beef and broccoli the next night.
- Cook a large serving of shredded chicken in your Instant Pot at the start of the week. That chicken can be dressed up with cumin and hot sauce for quesadillas, tossed with salad dressing atop greens, or thrown into a quick soup.
- Roast a full tray of veggies to use all week in omelets, on salads, or as pizza toppings for a make-your-own-pizza night.
- Leftover steak can be repurposed into Philly cheesesteak sandwiches.
- Leftover pizza dough can be used to make breakfast pizzas the next morning.
- Leftover pasta can be combined with a new, complementary sauce, veggies, and cheese and baked for a like-new pasta dish. This is especially delicious with ravioli!
- Extra rice can be combined with a few veggies, soy sauce, and eggs for a delicious and fast fried rice.

What are some ways your family likes to repurpose leftovers?

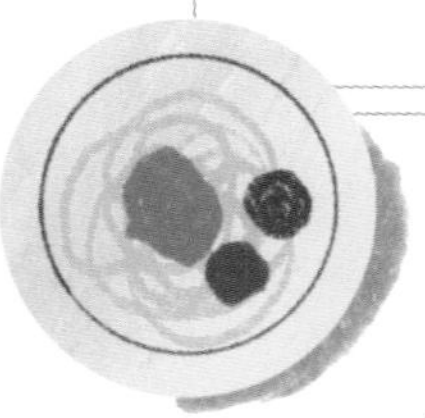

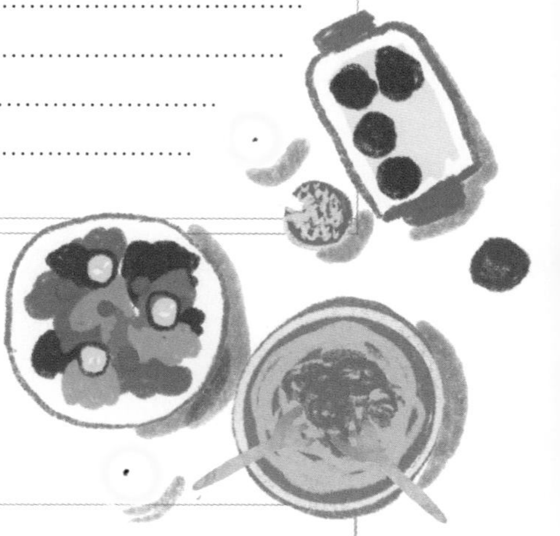

Cozy Tip

Ordering groceries has been a huge game changer for me. I know it's not for everyone, but if it's in your budget, do whatever is convenient for you and works for your lifestyle.

Also, always plan to double each recipe for leftovers you can eat the next day for lunch or dinner or freeze for Future You—she'll thank you!

NO. 57 COZY EATING FOR KIDS

Obviously, it's best if you can get your kids to eat what you eat, but if you're dealing with young children and toddlers, that may not be possible. Cope has been pretty good about new foods, but he has gone through picky phases just like every other kid. We've learned that dinnertime just isn't cozy if you spend the whole time arguing with your kid over the food on their plate.

Set a few ground rules (like each child must try one bite of everything) and then don't stress beyond that. As long as you keep presenting nourishing food and make your kids keep trying it, eventually their palates will open up. At each meal, offer at least one healthy food you know they like so they'll eat enough to be full, even if they refuse to eat anything else on the table.

Here are some ways I make my life easier cooking for picky kiddos:

- Cook taco meat, veggies, and beans separately so kiddos can customize.
- When making lasagna, prep all the ingredients, and then make a big pan for the adults with all the fixings you like and a small, plainer pan for the kids.
- Cook chicken noodle soup, ladle a cup of soup for your kid, then add herbs or lemon juice at the end. The herbs stay brighter and fresher, and your kiddo doesn't complain about green stuff in the soup!
- Have make-your-own nights: quesadillas, pizzas, and tacos are all easy to customize with items your child likes, and you can often sneak in a few healthy ingredients without their noticing!
- Get sneaky with veggies. I add extra veggies into lots of sauces, dressings, and dips and blend well so my child can't see exactly what he's eating. It's surprising how many flavors kids like just fine when they

can't see where those flavors come from.

- Find fun shapes. You can find pasta in different shapes and also use cookie cutters to present foods in different ways. These are great ideas to get a child to try something they might not otherwise.
- Dips! Kids love to dip things, and you can often get your child to try something new by dipping it into a sauce they already enjoy.

No. 58 July Home Maintenance Checklist

Sweet, sweet summertime! In Michigan, July is the month when summer finally arrives. I try to keep my maintenance list lighter in summer months so I can enjoy as much sunshine as possible. However, there are certain tasks that are easier to do during warm weather, and I keep a few indoor items on my list for stormy days or scorching-hot days when I'd rather be inside in the A/C.

JULY HOME MAINTENANCE CHECKLIST						
	Check all outdoor areas, bathrooms, and your laundry room for signs of mold. These spaces tend to be warmer, more humid, and are more prone to mold growth, especially in hot summer months.					
	Inspect sink, shower, and bath caulking for deterioration. Clean and repair as needed.					
	Reseal tile grout as needed.					
	Check your plumbing for any potential issues. You'll want to focus on dripping faucets, running toilets, signs of leaks, and your sump pump. Get a plumber out to fix anything you can't tackle yourself. This is also a great time to clean out your drains and clean shower heads and faucets well to remove build-up.					
	Vacuum the bathroom exhaust fan grill.					
	Vacuum the refrigerator and freezer coils. Empty and clean drip trays.					

	Repair or replace siding if needed.					
	Inspect exterior door hardware. Fix squeaky handles and loose locks.					
	Schedule an arborist to check the health of your trees. If needed, have trees trimmed, dead trees removed, and sick trees treated.					
	Deadhead flowers and bushes as needed and dig up weeds weekly. Water your plants often to protect them from the heat.					
	Clean out outdoor décor, along with outdoor and pool toys. Throw out anything that is beyond repair and look for replacements while stores have lots of inventory. Independence Day sales are a great time to stock up on fun outdoor items to make your summer days cozier and more fun.					
	Clean the garbage disposal.					
	Check your HVAC filters and change them as needed.					
	Vacuum your dryer's lint trap.					
	Check your water softener system.					
	Check the temperature on your water heater.					
	If you have pets, give them their monthly flea, tick, and heart guard medicines.					

No. 59 Get Outside

I live to be outside in the summer. Sunshine and warmth bring me so much joy physically, mentally, spiritually, and socially. I particularly love having friends and family over during the summer. One way we have found to make our outdoor spaces cozier is to treat them like additional, extended square footage of our home.

I've created seating outdoors so we can gather with friends and enjoy comfortable conversations in the garden, on the porch, or near the pool. I've treated these spaces the same way I would a room in my home, considering comfort, light, and aesthetics. If I didn't have natural shade, I added it with an easy-to-adjust umbrella. I added outdoor lighting for the evenings and put out candles and lanterns for more diffused light. I chose outdoor-friendly fabrics that are easy to clean and comfortable. I added throw pillows and blankets that can easily be brought out before a gathering.

The things you love and that make your home feel cozy and personalized also exist in outdoor-friendly versions. I've even brought my antiques outside, with both vintage garden iron furniture and antique-like patio furniture. I have plants scattered throughout my home, and I mimic that with smaller pots of herbs and florals scattered across my patios and in lots of outdoor nooks.

So get outside and make your outdoor spaces cozy, where you can enjoy spending time. It will make your home seem bigger and more relaxing, whether you have a whole yard or just a balcony or deck.

Cozy Tip

Rather than buying new, consider Craigslist, Facebook Marketplace, or local thrift and antique stores for finding outdoor furniture. You may find the bones of something wonderful and simply need to update some cushions. You can breathe life into repurposing something *and* save money.

No. 60 Outdoor Play

Kids need fresh air (and so do their parents!). Getting everyone outside opens a whole new world of play options. Kids really *can* play outside in almost any weather, so long as they have the right gear to keep them cool and hydrated or warm and cozy.

With their wild imaginations, kids can turn the smallest item into a chance to play, including sticks, pinecones, and rocks. But I've found that intentionally creating some cozy play spots for Cope has kept him busier and happier outdoors. A fun sprinkler, a watering can he can use to "help" water plants and make mud pies, and a water table have all been big hits. Throw some plastic water toys in a bucket and put those out with a water table or a kiddie pool for a day of water fun in the sun.

For little ones, it's so easy to create play bins that can be pulled out for a creativity injection. Sidewalk chalk, a small water gun for erasing, and some old rags in a bucket make for fun outdoor art options. A bin filled with bubbles and wands and some dress-up wings can help kids create a magical fairy garden in the backyard. A bucket for collecting pretty rocks, seeds, flowers, and leaves can live with construction paper, glue, and crayons for creating nature-inspired masterpieces. We love kinetic sand, and I always keep a tote handy with different types of paints, kid-friendly scissors, and craft paper for impromptu outdoor art sessions.

For older kids, toys like Hula-Hoops, jump ropes, and water guns are still super fun. If you have the budget and space for an outdoor playhouse or playset with swings and slides, it will last longer than you think. Sporty options like a basketball hoop, a soccer or field hockey goal, and plenty of balls to choose from will keep bigger kids happy and active too. Who knows, you may end up playing a little more yourself and making some wonderful family memories with so much fun stuff around!

No. 61 Kid-Specific Cozy

Home should always be a cozy, safe place for children, and their bedrooms should make them feel relaxed and at ease. When thinking about spaces for children, I keep in mind that kids grow up. I try to stick to classic, neutral elements for paint, flooring, furniture, bedding, and light fixtures—things that will grow with the child.

It's important to meet kids where they are, so try to use less expensive décor that can be changed over time as your child's tastes change. If your kid loves superheroes, a superhero toy, blanket, and pajamas are great options. Obsessed with princesses? Purchase some small, inexpensive princess toys you can style on shelves and the tops of dressers. Those things can easily be changed as your child moves on to other interests.

It's also important to think through how you want your child to use their space. Creating zones for reading and playing, with spots for books and toys at the child's level, will make the room more functional. We created special shelves for Cope that let him easily find his favorite books, and now we find that we read a lot more.

No matter how big or small, if you create a cozy space for your child to learn and grow, it will help you all to be happier at home.

Cozy Tip

Sometimes I need to remind myself that less really *is* more—and that's the case for kids too. I try to keep a limited number of toys for Cope so he can really enjoy them and not be overwhelmed by them. And bonus tip: a few cute bins to keep everything put away will make your home a more pleasant place for all of you.

Cozy Kid Room Checklist
Soft sheets
Warm blanket or quilt
Diffused lamp lighting
Nightlight
Speaker or noise machine for white noise
Ceiling projector for cozy, starry nights!

No. 62 Cozy Family Time

Having cozy family time is so important to me. I love having the chance to create beautiful memories with Cope and Jose as we intentionally prioritize our time together. I'm very aware that childhood lasts only so long, and I want to make these years count.

To us, cozy family time can be as simple as snuggling together in bed to read books before Cope goes to sleep or cooking pancakes together in the kitchen. They can be "fancier" events, like a movie night with themed snacks or playing *Candyland* with actual candy prizes. There's something magical about creating a little magic for your kids. Seeing Cope stare in awe at a sunrise as we walk around the farm or noticing how he watches the fireflies blinking while we go for a night swim reminds Jose and me of our own childhood wonder.

What are special ways you spend time together as a family?

....

....

Is there a new family tradition you've been wanting to try with your kids, like game night or movie night?

....

....

Does your family have specific holiday traditions? Why do you think they are such hits?

....

....

Have you planned any future "family time" activities to do together for when your kids are a little older?

....

....

Are there family activities you miss from when your kids were younger? Could they be changed a little to work now?

....

....

Ask your kids about their favorite way to spend time as a family. How can you make more time for those things?

....

....

....

....

No. 63

August Home Maintenance Checklist

It's tough to focus on getting anything done when the sun is shining and I'd rather swim, work in the garden, and spend the evenings grilling and roasting s'mores over the fire pit. But August is often the warmest month of the year, and the heat always reminds me to take care of tasks that help to prevent fires around our home. It's also a good time to check for water issues ahead of the cold winters. Luckily, these tasks don't take much time, which means you will still have plenty of time to enjoy the last few days of summer sun and fun.

AUGUST HOME MAINTENANCE CHECKLIST						
	Clean your kitchen exhaust fan filter.					
	Clean your refrigerator and freezer coils. Empty and clean drip trays.					
	Give your refrigerator and freezer a good scrub, both inside and outside. Remove any expired or unused food and condiments.					
	Check your dishwasher for leaks and clean its filter.					
	Look for leaks around kitchen and bathroom sinks and cabinets, as well as toilets.					
	Inspect the water heater for leaks.					
	Test fire extinguishers and each of your ground fault circuit interrupters.					
	Check all lamps, electronics, and appliances for frayed cords and wires.					

	Vacuum heat registers and heat vents.					
	Have your dryer lint trap and ductwork professionally cleaned to prevent blockages and fires. This is especially important if you have a very long duct.					
	Check that indoor and outdoor air vents are not blocked.					
	If applicable, oil your garage-door opener and chain, as well as garage door hinges.					
	Clean the garbage disposal.					
	Check your HVAC filters and change them as needed.					
	Vacuum your dryer's lint trap.					
	Check your water softener system.					
	Check the temperature on your water heater.					
	If you have pets, give them their monthly flea, tick, and heart guard medicines.					

No. 64 Cozy Recipe for Game Night

My favorite food to serve at a game or movie night is a board that matches the theme of our event. There's just something *fun* about food arranged on a board! From adults to kids, we all get into it. Depending on the event, you could provide a snack, a dessert, or an easy grab-and-eat dinner.

In the summer, we host pool playdates on Saturdays with friends, and this is our go-to dinner. We switch up the board, but we always hit the same categories—a cheese, a meat, some fruit, a jam or spread, and some delicious crackers or breads. We usually serve it alongside a veggie tray as well. I can make the board as simple or as elaborate as I want based on whatever I happen to have on hand, and everyone loves it.

I've done a board of sandwiches arranged with chips and pickles. A board with crackers, cheese, and charcuterie with the crackers arranged like squares on a board game. A board with sliders, French fries, and little bowls filled with ketchup, mustard, pickles, and other burger toppings. Dessert boards are always a hit too—boards of everything needed for gourmet s'mores or boards of nostalgic candy. I've even seen people hop on the butter board trend and serve spreads of soft, seasoned butter served alongside warm, crusty bread. (Listen, don't knock it 'til you've tried it—butter boards can be delicious!)

Easy, fun, and with usually little cooking involved, boards are the best!

What kind of board could you make for a movie you love?

....

....

No. 65 Favorite Cozy Kids' Books

One of my favorite things about children's books is how much color, life, and beauty they can add to kids' bedrooms and playrooms. In Cope's room, we added DIY book ledges to display our favorites face-out so we can find them easily for our nightly story time and so we can enjoy the whimsical art too! The book ledges are also a great place to decorate with seasonal garlands and other small items that keep Cope's room fun.

Our favorite books for babies

Goodnight Moon by Margaret Wise Brown

On the Night You Were Born by Nancy Tillman

God Bless You and Good Night by Hannah C. Hall

The Very Hungry Caterpillar by Eric Carle

Any of the *Little Golden Books*

Our favorite books for toddlers

We Belong to Each Other by Liz Marie and Jose Galvan

(I know I'm biased, but I love the book Jose and I wrote together. The kiddos in our lives have all loved it too!)

Knuffle Bunny by Mo Willems

The Rabbit Listened by Cori Doerrfeld

The Bad Seed series by Jory John

The Tale of Peter Rabbit by Beatrix Potter

Our Favorite Books for Bigger Kids

Dragons Love Tacos by Adam Rubin

Sleepy, the Goodnight Buddy by Drew Daywalt

The Mouse and the Motorcycle by Beverly Cleary

Dream Big for Kids by Bob Goff and Lindsey Goff Viducich

How to Make Friends with a Ghost by Rebecca Green

Your Favorites

No. 66 Kids' Clothes

One thing no one prepared me for about motherhood is how often I'd need to clean out Cope's closet! I knew kids grow fast, but I didn't *know*—you know? It seems like every few months, another adorable shirt or pair of pants doesn't fit anymore, and I realize I need to go through his drawers and hanging space to pull out what doesn't fit and figure out what I need to buy next.

Something about that process is emotional in a way I wasn't fully prepared for either. When he outgrows clothes or a toy, or when he switches to a new interest, it's fun to see how he's growing, and I get excited about all the new that he's into. But folding and putting away a too-small outfit for the last time really tugs on my heart strings. It's a physical reminder that he is growing up *so fast,* and I have shed more than a few tears cleaning out his closet. I get why some moms hold onto baby clothes far past the chance to use them again. Those tiny booties and too-small T-shirts hold so many memories. That makes them really difficult to part with.

Still, Cope is growing all the time, and he needs new clothes whether it makes me sentimental or not. One thing that helps me is to keep a running list of his sizes in the Notes app on my phone. That way, I can always see which size he is now, and when I spot something cool or find a great deal, I can make a solid guess at what size he'll need for the next season.

Even though it makes me sad, I clean out his closet regularly. I donate anything I'm not attached to, and I'm often able to sell the more expensive things I've bought for him on local parenting sites or in consignment shops. I also save anything I really love just in case, sometime in the future, I'm blessed with the chance to use it again for another little one who will call me Mama and grow up too fast.

Cozy Tip

Let yourself keep a few precious things you want to save or things you might want to use for another child. Bins and labels are your friends here. But try not to save more than you have the space for, or the volume of stuff will become too much.

No. 67 Cozy Clean

I certainly don't keep a perfectly clean home, but I have found a few ways to make keeping things tidy easier for me and my family, and I hope they work for you too.

- Tidy up every night or every morning. Grab a laundry basket and walk through the house; use the basket to carry items to the correct rooms and put them away.
- Keep your cleaning essentials in plain view. I am a big advocate for purchasing attractive, heirloom quality basics for brooms, mops, dustbins, and other cleaning items. I hang mine in the mudroom. They act as décor, and seeing them reminds me to clean!
- Put your cleaning sprays in pretty bottles and keep them in one place that you access often so you see them regularly. Using glass spray bottles means I use less plastic, and I enjoy cleaning more.
- Label bins, shelves, and other containers around your house. Whether they're subtle or not, labels can help everyone in your house put things away quickly and easily.
- Setting a family or roommate cleaning routine is a great way to delegate and make sure everyone is doing their share. Get a chart or some pieces of paper and begin to divide up your tasks.
- It's okay to ask for help. At times, I've needed to ask family, friends, or neighbors to help with a big project or simply to help me catch up when I've fallen behind. If you have the budget, hiring someone to come even once a month can be a huge help. When life gets hard or hectic, it's easy to put off things like tidying and

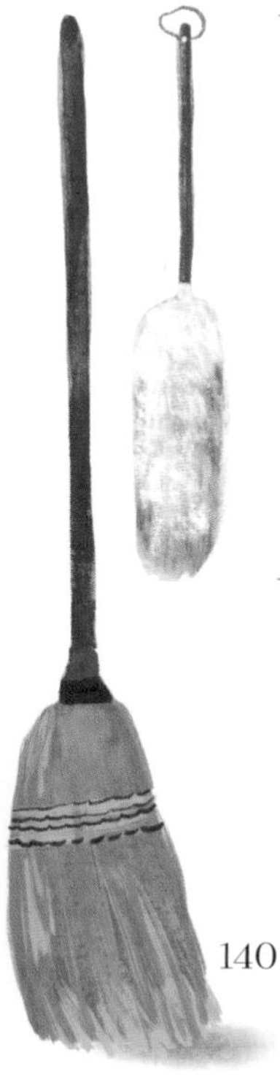

cleaning. But having your house feel put together will make you feel a lot more peaceful even if everything else in life is chaotic.

- Create a cleaning schedule to tackle a few items each day. This way, it doesn't feel so overwhelming to keep the house clean.
- Don't count out those littles. Give them age-appropriate tasks, and before you know it, even the smallest kids will be able to do things on their own (which is a really important life skill to learn!).
- When each season changes, set aside a few hours to put away seasonal items you no longer need and get out items for the season ahead. This will corral clutter and help you feel more prepared.
- After you clean or tidy a room, give it a spritz with your favorite spray or light that candle in the room. It's a cozy finishing touch that will help keep you motivated as you work.

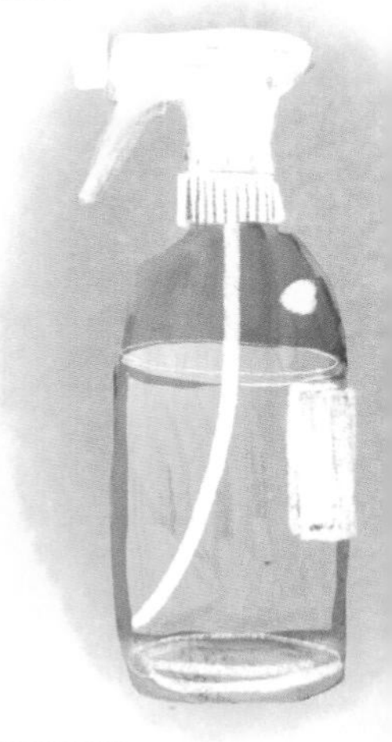

What are your personal cleaning pain points? What always feels messy? What's a chore that always feels like a hate?

....

....

....

How can you delegate those tasks or make them easier to accomplish?

....

....

....

Tomorrow we'll work on a cleaning schedule to help you get going!

No. 68 Cleaning Schedules

Sticking to daily, weekly, and monthly cleaning schedules has been a game changer at our house. We have help come every couple of weeks, but having a routine helps hold Jose and me accountable and keeps any task from piling up for too long.

Here is my personal cleaning schedule and a list of the things I do every day, week, and every month. Hopefully it will give you some ideas for creating a cleaning schedule that works for you and your family.

Monday:

- Collect trash throughout the house.
- Take trash and recycling to the curb.

Tuesday:

- Wipe down appliances and electronics.
- Do a quick clean of Cope's toys and play areas.

Wednesday:

- Water all the plants in the house and wipe down their leaves. (I call this "Water Wednesdays!")
- Dust and wipe down shelves, décor, and blinds.

Thursday:

- Change and wash sheets and other bedding so the beds are ready for weekend naps (and maybe, if we are lucky, the chance to sleep in a little!).

Friday:

- Clean out and wipe down car interiors.
- Wash cars, if needed.

Saturday:

- Tackle any remaining cleaning tasks around the house.

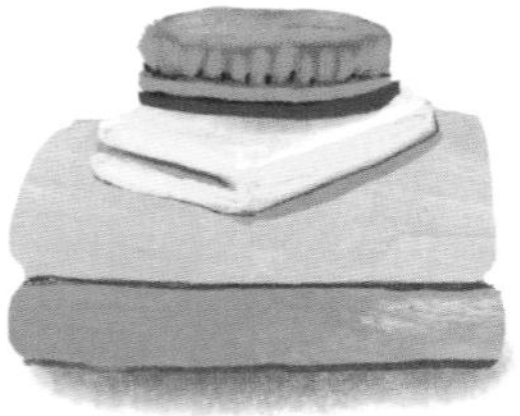

Sunday:

- Wipe down bathrooms.
- Vacuum and steam mop wood floors.

Daily:

- Run the dishwasher.
- Do a quick kitchen cleanup.
- Put in a load of laundry: wash, dry, and put away.

Weekly:

- Change and wash sheets.
- Do a quick clean of bathrooms (including toilets, showers, tubs, countertops, and sinks).
- Vacuum rugs.
- Sweep floors.
- Dust shelves and electronics.
- Scrub kitchen counters and sink.
- Wipe down the outside of the refrigerator.
- Wipe down stovetop burners.
- Wipe down doorknobs and light switches.
- Water plants and dust leaves.

Monthly:

- Polish floors.
- Dust fan blades and blinds.
- Wipe down baseboards and trim.
- Wipe down cabinet faces.
- Clean out the refrigerator and give all shelves and drawers a good scrub.
- Dust and wipe down pantry and cabinet shelves.
- Clean the oven.
- Thoroughly clean stovetop burners.
- Tidy and dust closet shelves.
- Wash quilts, duvets, duvet covers, pillow shams, and pillows.
- Wash throws, blankets, and slipcovers.
- Wipe down trash cans, inside and out.

Think about what your home needs. Tomorrow, we'll create a customized plan just for you!

No. 69

Customizable Cleaning Schedule

MONDAY

TUESDAY

WEDNESDAY

THURSDAY

FRIDAY

SATURDAY

SUNDAY

WEEKLY

MONTHLY

No. 70 The Perfect Cleaning Cupboard

If you'd like to upgrade your cleaning cupboard with beautiful but utilitarian, heirloom-quality items, here are my must-haves. These aren't always easy to find, nor are they especially inexpensive, but they are durable, work well, and make cleaning a lot more fun.

- Brooms: All of my brooms have colored, wooden handles with quality bristles. I have a standard broom for inside the house, a hard-bristled option for tackling big messes, and a barn broom I use for our patio.
- Metal dustpan: I found mine at an antique store, and I hang it in my mudroom with my brooms. It's pretty, so I don't mind having it out in the open and accessible, and it works better than plastic.
- Glass spray bottles: I fill these with my favorite cleaning solutions. Having all my bottles the same size and weight is helpful for keeping myself organized, plus they look better in a cabinet or on a shelf.
- Mops: I have several mop options for different chores: an automated option that allows me to fill it with my favorite cleaning solution, a standard cotton-bottom mop, and another sturdy option for cleaning outdoor spaces.
- Duster: I use an antique feather duster, which I find for sale in antique shops. They cost little, and they work really well.
- Microfiber cloths: I use these for everything from dusting to scrubbing. They're versatile and keep me from using too many paper towels!
- Vacuum with a HEPA filter: We love our animals, but we don't love allergens. A lightweight vacuum with a HEPA filter cleans up all the pet and farm animal dander and gets rid of pollen.

- Wet vacuum: I use this for stubborn messes like mud that gets tracked into rugs or when food and drinks are spilled onto my upholstered pieces. I'm always so glad to have it when I need it.
- Sponges: I keep a variety of sponges stocked for washing dishes, scrubbing down our bathrooms, and tackling other messes. I have gentle ones, medium ones, and steel wool for when I need more power.
- Scrub brush: Mine has a wooden handle and stiff, high-quality bristles. Every two to three months, I fill a bucket with water and ammonia, grab my scrub brush, and get down on my hands and knees to give my floors a good scrub.
- Metal buckets: I use these for storage and cleaning. They are so versatile, and I don't worry about them cracking as long as I take good care of them.
- Multipurpose steamer: I use this for so many things: steam cleaning floors, pressing slipcovers and curtains, and even cleaning windows.

No. 71 September Home Maintenance Checklist

September always feels like a fresh start to me. I think we're conditioned to feel that way, thanks to all the years we spend in school. If you have kids, back-to-school time means new teachers, new friendships, and aisle upon aisle of brand-new notebooks and pencils. I love that new-paper smell! And if you aren't a parent, fall is still an excellent time for a fresh start as you pack away spring and summer items and get cozy for the chillier days ahead. So break out the pumpkin spice candles and use this list to get your home ready for fall!

SEPTEMBER HOME MAINTENANCE CHECKLIST						
	Check your outdoor lights and replace any burnt-out bulbs.					
	If you have a septic system, check for signs of trouble while the ground is still soft. Every three to five years, have a professional inspect and pump the tank.					
	Have your chimney cleaned and inspected so it's ready for cozy fires.					
	Get your furnace and ductwork serviced before turning on the heat for the season.					
	Test your thermostats to ensure they're working properly.					
	For homes heated with steam heat, call the plumber for your boiler's annual checkup and have the water drained to remove sediment. Also, have the plumber check your radiators to make sure the valves are working properly and haven't worn out.					

	Spruce up your home for fall. Give the whole house a good scrub: baseboards, blinds, floors, and furniture. If you live in a cooler climate, reverse the settings on your fans to clockwise to pull cool air up so your home stays warmer.					
	Clean and pack away summer décor and set up fall décor.					
	Pick up local gourds and pumpkins for your porch later in the month.					
	Plant fall flowers like marigolds, mums, and dahlias in your pots and beds for a pop of autumn color.					
	Reseed your lawn, if needed.					
	Plant perennials like peonies and hydrangeas as well as bulbs for tulips and daffodils so they have time to get established before blooming in the spring.					
	As soon as the air turns chilly, winterize your pool by cleaning and covering it for the season. Clean and pack away pool toys and other swim-specific equipment.					
	Clean the garbage disposal.					
	Check your HVAC filters and change them as needed.					
	Vacuum your dryer's lint trap.					
	Check your water softener system.					
	Check the temperature on your water heater.					
	If you have pets, give them their monthly flea, tick, and heart guard medicines.					

No. 72 Knowing Your Fabrics

When you're out shopping, having a swatch of fabric you've used for draperies, throw pillows, slipcovers, or anything else on hand can be a life saver! You are far less likely to come home with something that clashes if you go out armed with swatches.

Flip to the back to the Cozy Home Guide. Gather your swatches and tape them on the marked page for reference. We also have an area for keeping track of the dimensions of your throw pillows. This will make it easy to purchase new covers for them or pick up fabric to make your own.

If you don't have any swatches, don't stress. You can take photos of the fabrics in your house and use those as you shop, although it's a little trickier to see colors accurately in photos. Another option is to look on the bottom of your upholstered furniture to see if there is any excess fabric that you can trim and use as a swatch. Curtains with deep hems often have a little extra fabric you can trim away as well. Unzip throw pillow covers and check the inside hems to see if there is a little extra you can cut away. Many companies that make rugs and pillows will let you order a swatch for a few dollars, so that's an option if you purchased one of those items recently.

Under each swatch, jot down the best method for cleaning that fabric. You might think you'll remember, but you won't—take it from me.

In the future, when you purchase new upholstered furniture, always ask for a swatch or two to keep on hand for reference. Once you get in the habit, you'll find it's so helpful, you'll never go back!

No
69
FINDING JOY
IN IT ALL
I hope you are sitting down somewhere while you are reading this. I hope it's cozy, I hope you are content, and I hope you are ready for the questions I'm about to ask. Look around you. Does everything in your home bring you joy? Does it help or benefit you and your family members? Or does it cause chaos and annoyance while contributing to clutter and mess? I know, that was a lot of questions, but they are so important to ask yourself as you assess your cozy home.
I may not be able to shed much wisdom from my thirty years of living, but I do know one thing from experience: Stuff causes stress. More stuff brings on more stress. More stuff doesn't mean more joy. Joy is loving everything that surrounds you and cozy is finding joy in everything and everyone in your home.
The process of decluttering is simple, but let me share a few tips that have helped me feel lighter, cozier, and happier in our home.
1. Do you need the item to assist your family for your daily needs? Does the item provide your home with joy from an assistance standpoint?
2. Do you love the item? Does the item give you joy when you look at it or use it? No? Toss it, donate it, or sell it.
3. Could a simple change make the item better? Could you paint the item, add something to the item, or move the item to a different room to make you love it more?
Those are questions I've asked myself as I've walked our entire home, from closets to bedrooms to our living quarters to our kitchen, and I can't believe what a weight it has taken off of me to rid our home of unwanted and unloved items. It has truly made our home cozier to have around only items that we love. Learning to find joy in it all is one of the biggest steps to making your home the coziest it can be.
154
P. CO

No. 73 DIY Ways to Freshen Up

There's something so comforting about a home that smells cozy. As much as I love candles and diffusers, sometimes a little DIY can be even better.

Stovetop Simmer Potpourri Recipe

This is my go-to around the holidays because it is so easy and has such a strong impact. Feel free to experiment with your favorite scents.

Ingredients

2 cups of sturdy fruit like cranberries or apples
Some citrus fruit like sliced oranges, lemons, or limes (you can also just use the peels)
Fresh or dried herbs and spices like vanilla (beans or extract), cinnamon sticks, rosemary, mint, thyme, cloves, or allspice
Seasonal options like pine needles, pumpkin spice blend, lavender, or flower petals
A few drops of your favorite essential oils

Instructions

1. Place your ingredients in a large pot, cover with water, set the heat to low, and gently simmer. That's it. No stirring or babysitting is needed (other than the occasional check for fire safety or to see if more water is needed). I let mine simmer for two to three hours at a time and set an alarm to make sure I remember to turn the stove off. The scent lasts all day.
2. Pour your blend into a mason jar and keep it in the fridge for up to a week. When you want to use it again, pour it into a clean pot, add more water, and let it simmer all over again.

DIY Room Spray

For a quick, nontoxic way to make any room smell great organically, make this simple DIY room spray.

Instructions

1. Find a spray bottle of your choice. (I love amber bottles.)
2. Add witch hazel or rubbing alcohol to the spray bottle for the base.
3. Add your favorite essential oils. (I love lavender on its own, but sometimes I like to mix it up with sandalwood, sweet orange, rosemary, bergamot, and more. Go with whatever combo of scents *you* like best.)
4. Give the bottle a good shake to combine the oils with the witch hazel.
5. Top off with water, leaving a little room at the top.
6. Give the bottle a shake each time before you use it.

NO. 74 Cleaning Challenges

There are certain things that are just hard to keep clean. Here's how I tackle those items that aren't easy but still need to be freshened up from time to time.

- Bed pillows: Synthetic bed pillows can be washed regularly in the washing machine with your normal detergent. For down pillows, wash every few months in the washing machine with a gentle detergent, like one for wool or silk, on the delicate cycle then dry them with a few tennis balls on low. They'll come out clean, fluffy, and smelling fresh.
- Throw pillows with covers: Remove covers and wash the pillows and covers separately. This allows you to get the pillow inserts very clean in your washing machine. Wash the covers in whatever way will keep them looking great the longest, be it hand washing, machine washing on gentle, or even dry cleaning.
- Throw pillows without covers: The filling in throw pillows can always be washed in the washing machine, but the same isn't always true of the casing. A good rule of thumb is to wash based on the material of the cover. If you have a silk pillow, for example, wash on delicate with a gentle detergent recommended for silks then hang to dry and fluff on ultralow with dryer balls.
- Upholstered furniture without slipcovers: If you don't have a wet vacuum, I suggest you get one just for cleaning upholstered pieces. You always want to do a spot check of your cleaning solution on a low-visible area, just to make sure it won't stain or discolor your upholstery. But if your spot check goes well, just follow the instructions for your wet vacuum. It'll leave your upholstery looking good as new! If you have kids or pets and don't like the look of slipcovers, I highly recommend getting your upholstered

pieces protected by a professional. It will save you tons of time and headaches when it comes to stains.

- Large-scale slipcovers: I love, love, love my slipcovers, but they aren't the easiest to wash, especially the larger ones. I always choose easy-wash fabrics for my slipcovers so I can use my washing machine. However, if you don't have a large-capacity washing machine, I recommend going to a laundromat to use their larger washers. If you don't have one nearby, you can hand-scrub your slipcovers in a utility sink or your bathtub with some detergent. Once clean, dry your slipcover on low, but remove it from the dryer while it's slightly damp. It's much easier to get back onto your furniture if it's not completely dry.
- Rugs: Your wet vacuum will be your most useful tool for removing stains from your rugs. You can clean a whole rug with your wet vac, but it could take quite a while. If you have several large rugs, it's probably worth hiring a carpet cleaning company to come in and clean them once a year.

No. 75 October Home Maintenance Checklist

As the weather turns colder, my list switches to preparing my home for the upcoming winter. The beginning of October is usually still warm enough to tackle outdoor tasks, so I prioritize those. Once the snow starts to fall, there will be plenty of time for indoor chores.

OCTOBER HOME MAINTENANCE CHECKLIST						
	Clean leaves and debris from gutters and downspouts. For cooler climates, do this early in the month before the first snows. For warmer climates, do this around Halloween.					
	Insulate outdoor faucets then clean and put away hoses and sprinklers for the year.					
	Insulate pipes in unheated areas of your home like the attic, garage, or crawl space.					
	If you have an irrigation system, turn it off and have it winterized.					
	For wood-burning fireplaces, stock up on seasoned firewood. Stack it loosely on pallets, and cover it with plastic sheeting to keep it dry and fungus-free.					
	Check your windows and doors for drafts. Caulk drafty door and window frames.					
	Install storm windows and the glass panel on storm doors to keep in the heat and keep out the cold.					

	Spray for insects. As the temperatures drop, bugs will be looking for heat!						
	Once the leaves have fallen, it's the perfect time to plant new trees and hardy shrubs so they will be ready to shoot up in the spring.						
	Prep your garden space for upcoming snows. This may mean moving vulnerable potted plants inside or under cover.						
	Clean and cover (or put away) your grill for the winter.						
	Clean and cover (or put away) your outdoor furniture and equipment too delicate to be left in the elements, like fountains and pots.						
	Clean and pack away summer-specific tools and equipment like your lawn mower, edger, weed eater, hedge trimmer, and the like.						
	Clean the garbage disposal.						
	Check your HVAC filters and change them as needed.						
	Vacuum your dryer's lint trap.						
	Check your water softener system.						
	Check the temperature on your water heater.						
	If you have pets, give them their monthly flea, tick, and heart guard medicines.						

No. 76 Clean and Pet-Friendly

I adore my pets. I can't imagine life without them, but I *could* live without some of the messes they make.

- Pet hair and fur: A vacuum cleaner with a HEPA filter is going to be your best friend. Make sure you get one with settings that work for the flooring you have in your home. Consider one made specifically for pets that shed. Having pets means you need to vacuum more frequently. If you hate vacuuming but love your pets, a robot vacuum may be a good solution.
- Potty messes and vomit: It's essential to clean these up as soon as possible because the protein and acid in these types of messes can damage certain materials, and the longer they sit, the worse the damage gets. For carpeting and rugs, a pet-specific cleaner with enzymes is best. A wet vacuum is crucial for cleaning up these messes from carpets and rugs, while a steam mop is a great tool for tile. For hardwoods, clean and disinfect quickly with a hardwood-safe floor cleaner. If odors linger, Febreze the area to lift up any bacteria clinging to soft surfaces.
- Nail and chew marks: If you have a pet that loves to gnaw on your wood furniture, it's best to stop that habit right away. Pet-safe but not-great-tasting furniture polish should be applied to the legs of your furniture every few days to keep your pets from destroying them. Pet nails can also leave marks on hardwood floors. Wood conditioner and polish can keep those marks from being super noticeable.
- Stains from bones, food, and treats: For anything that can go in the washing machine, stain remover and detergent with enzymes can take out most of these stains, along with some scrubbing before you throw it in the wash. For carpeting or rugs, the same enzyme-based cleaners that work for potty messes and vomit work wonders for these stains too.

The Artist & the Garden

No. 77 A Cozy Home Office Space

People around the world have seen a huge need for home office space. We're fortunate that this old farm has rooms and buildings we've been able to update and use for offices and other workspaces. If that's not an option for you, here are some ways to create flexible but cozy home office spaces:

- Use a guest room as a hybrid office and guest space.
- Transform a large closet into a desk area.
- Find a quiet corner of a family room or bonus room to set up a cozy work corner.
- Consider a dining room or other space you rarely use that could be reborn as an office.

Here are a few things to keep in mind when creating a home office space:

- Don't set up your office in a high-traffic area; you'll be distracted and frustrated by interruptions.
- Find a pretty view, whether it's a window or a lovely part of your house. If you're facing unfinished chores or projects, it might be hard to focus.
- Save up for a comfortable chair that you want to see *and* sit in. If it takes a while to afford this piece, investigate supportive desk chair cushions that will help you until you can save up.
- Consider understated standing desks, keyboard trays, and other items that will help you ergonomically but will still fit into your cozy décor (or that's easy to tuck away!).
- Make your space beautiful by surrounding yourself with plants, inspiring art, family photos, and other items that bring you peace.

What's on your cozy office wish list?

No. 78 Seasonal Organizing

Switching up décor with the seasons adds cozy vibes to your home, but storing all those items and keeping them organized can be challenging. I love decorating for each holiday, but it's never as much fun to put things away at the end of the season. How and where you store items will depend upon your home, but I do have some tips to make things easier, whether you stash your stuff in an attic, basement, shed, or closet.

- Use clear bins with lids designed for stacking. It is *far* easier to find what you're looking for in clear bins. I'm not suggesting you run out and buy clear bins right this second, but I would recommend upgrading to clear bins over time. Measure your storage space and shelves to figure out which sizes of bins would work best. Put those measurements into the Notes app on your phone. If you spot a great deal on clear bins while you're shopping, you can grab the ones you need. Look online to find options you love and set a price alert to tell you when they go on sale. Just make sure you buy bins with sturdy lids designed for stacking.
- Label the bins. This is so simple, but there were many years I didn't label things well. I thought I would remember what was in each box. Spoiler alert: I did not! So learn from me and label each bin by holiday/season and the basics of what's inside, like "Christmas: Lights" or "Easter: Baskets." You can write on bins using an oil-based paint pen, or use a label maker for removeable labels. If you're storing bins where they will be seen often, it may be worth upgrading your label maker to one that can cut out removable vinyl to make labels that match your décor.
- Include a manifest. Once you have your seasonal décor packed to your liking, take a few minutes to write down what's inside each on separate

pieces of paper. Tape the paper to the inside of the lid so when it's time to repack everything, you can put things away where they fit best without having to play *Tetris* with your stuff every season.

- Wipe down items before putting them away. Wash linens, blankets, slipcovers, and throw pillows. Wipe down decorations and give outdoor items a good scrub before packing them away. Remove batteries so they don't erode and explode inside your items (yes, this actually happens!). This is also a good time to test anything that uses electricity, like strings of lights. The end of the season is a great time to pick up décor and lights on sale, so it's worth checking before packing everything up.
- Have a few empty bins ready to go. I always end up buying a few new items for décor each season. Having a few empty bins ready to go makes it easy for me to store the new items.

Cozy Tip

If you want to be super organized, you can take things a step further. We have a lot of décor, so we've had to up our storage organization game. These days, not only do we label our bins on the outside and add a manifest inside, but we also give the bin a name (i.e., "Fall Box 1") in our storage database along with a description of what's inside (we like Google Sheets because it can be accessed from anywhere and it's easy to use). The database is searchable, so those descriptions make it easy for us to find something specific quickly. We also include a photo of what's in each box and a photo of where each box is stored. These photos are so helpful when you have others helping you, because what someone may call a wreath, someone else may think of as a garland.

NO. 79 General Organization

It's much easier to live the cozy life when you can quickly and easily find what you need when you need it. It sounds so boring, but having your home well organized really adds to the cozy vibes. How many times have you purchased something only to find you already had that item? Have you ever spent a hectic half hour searching everywhere for something you needed? I'm not the only one, right?

Your closets and shelves don't need to look like you hired a professional organizer, but it's worth taking the time to create zones for certain items so your home stays tidy. Zones in your closet make getting ready easier, and zones in the pantry and refrigerator make it easier to assess what you have before grocery shopping. I keep boxes of pasta in the same spot alongside jars of tomato sauce. Baking supplies are all together

on one shelf. And I keep all my glasses together in one cabinet and all my bowls in another.

Zones are especially crucial if you have kids. Kids can't help you keep things tidy if they don't know where things go. Having a zone for bags and shoes and coats makes it simple for little ones to know where to put their jacket and boots when they come in the door. A zone for toys means your toddler can help with cleaning up his toys. A zone for craft supplies will keep you from finding glue sticks and pom-poms all over the house.

I love baskets and decorative boxes. These are great for organizing items by category, plus they look great too. A tangle of chargers can look messy on the counter, but a pretty basket hides them from sight while keeping them within easy reach. Pretty boxes look nice when they're styled on shelves (and they hold more than you'd think!).

Labels are huge for keeping things organized. A label maker is great for making labels that are easy to remove inside of drawers and on cabinet shelves. Having that visual reminder of what goes where helps me to put things back where they belong.

Dividers and trays will help you make the most of each space. Drawer and shelf dividers can help you create zones within a cabinet or dresser. And organizing trays help corral smaller items within bigger spaces. Old shoe boxes or well-washed food containers are great for this. Wrap boxes in pretty paper, and you would never know they used to hold Nikes. A little spray paint can disguise jars that used to hold nuts or olives.

I am always on the lookout for great deals on baskets, bins, trays, and other organizing essentials. When I find some that are my style or on a great sale, I add them to my collection. I think the biggest mistake we all make is thinking we have to get our entire homes organized all at once. That is way too much for anyone to tackle! Start small—one shelf or drawer at a time—until you complete that room. Then move to the next. Using that method, I've been able to get most of our rooms organized over time, and it has made our lives so much more peaceful. I wish that same peace for you.

NO. 80 REGULAR EDITING

One of the biggest misconceptions about getting your home organized is that it's a one-and-done process. We all go through seasons when we need different things and have different routines. The way our homes are organized has to grow and shift with our needs, which means you'll need to edit and reorganize as time goes by.

I can admit that I'm never going to be a minimalist, but that doesn't mean I need to hold on to everything I've ever owned just in case I may need it someday. "Editing" my things regularly helps me make room for new finds, which is important because my style is always evolving and so are my family's needs. I'm sure the same is true for you.

As a newlywed, you shift your home to make room for your spouse's stuff. When you have little ones, you need more toy storage in the family room and maybe a cabinet to hold sippy cups, bottles, and snack cups. With older kids, you need files for schoolwork and spots to hold sports equipment. To make room for the new, you need to get rid of the old and adjust where and how those things are stored.

Each new season, I take a little time to edit our clothes and accessories and Cope's toys. I throw out anything that's broken, torn, or can't be fixed. Then I donate anything that's still serviceable and sell items that were a larger investment so that I can buy replacements or new items we need. I also edit holiday-specific or seasonal items before I pack them away at the end of each season. That way, I'm not storing something all year that I don't plan to use again. And every few years, I go through the same process with things like our regular décor, books, and linens.

Every month, I go through our pantry and fridge to make sure we get rid of expired items or things we no longer eat. Items that aren't expired but won't get used go to a food bank. After my fridge and pantry edit, I have space for the items we actually eat. I also clean out our drawer of plastic and

paper bags, our stash of water bottles, and my collection of kitchen tools and serving pieces.

Our farm animals are a big help with keeping our kitchen decluttered. Apples, bananas, and other fruit we're unable to eat go to the sheep and alpacas. If you find yourself with a surplus of fruit or vegetables that you can't eat quickly enough, check with local farms to see if any will take extra items for their animals.

It would feel overwhelming to try to do all of that in one burst of frantic organizing. I find it far easier to work on editing a little at a time throughout the year. If I have ten minutes to kill, I can quickly edit a cabinet or a bin of toys. Thirty minutes? I tackle the coat closet. An hour? Cope's closet and drawers. Sticking to short periods of time makes organizing feel less like work. To make it even more fun, I will usually listen to my favorite music or an audiobook. Making editing part of my regular routine has made organizing much more manageable and has made it possible for me to *stay* organized, which is a win in my book.

No. 81 Cozy Budgeting

I'm not a financial expert, but I think budgeting is an important part of curating a cozy home. Living within your means makes your life so much easier and calmer; stressing about money will rob you of your peace, which is decidedly *not* cozy.

Contrary to what you may see on social media, you don't have to have new or perfectly decorated rooms to have a peaceful, lovely home. You do not have to spend a ton of money to create a loving haven for your family. Get inspired by social media, but don't feel like you have to spend like someone else. Styling my home and sharing it online is part of my job, but I'm not going into debt to do it. Here are some things we do to stay on track:

- Budgeting: Budgeting is key when it comes to decorating and organizing your home. Jose and I do our research and set a realistic budget before we start any project, including comparing what different things cost. We DIY what we can to save money, but we also know when it's worth it to hire a pro, and we budget for that. Sometimes that means we do a less expensive, temporary fix while we save up to do what we really want. Waiting isn't fun, but to us, it's worth it to wait instead of taking

on debt. We contribute money from every paycheck into a home fund, even if we don't have a specific project or purchase in mind. That way, when we decide on a project or find that *perfect* piece of furniture while we're shopping, we have the money for it.

- Shop smart: We also shop around. I don't buy full price if I can help it, and I also try to buy out of season as much as possible. Holiday decorations cost the most before the holiday, but you can get bargains at the end of the season if you are willing to hunt for them. The same is true of outdoor furniture and décor. Shop in the fall and winter for best deals.
- Sell, sell, sell: Because I change up my décor so often, I have gotten in the habit of selling things I no longer need or want. There are many options online for selling to others in your community. Even if you price your items on the low side, that's money you can add to your home budget for buying décor you want or putting toward a renovation.

I know it's not fun to think about money (especially when it feels like you never have enough). But I want to encourage you to do it even when it's uncomfortable, because setting realistic budgets and sticking to them is so worth it for the peace of mind alone. It also forces you to get creative, and I've gotten some of my best ideas thinking outside of the box to stay within budget. Creating a beautiful and cozy home doesn't have to be expensive or stressful to achieve. It may take some waiting and planning, but to me, that makes the day you complete the renovation even more fun!

Cozy Tip

Try not to compare, whether in your real life or on social media. There will always be someone who makes more or has more. But that doesn't mean you can't find joy and contentment in your own cozy haven, however big or humble it may be.

NO. 82 TACKLING PROJECTS

I love DIY. There's something so special and rewarding about looking at something you made or decorated with your own two hands, especially when it comes out just as good as or even better than it was in your head. DIY is a great option when you really want something but it's outside your budget. When you're willing to roll up your sleeves and get your hands dirty, you can do a lot with a little money. I also love DIY because whatever you make will *absolutely* be one-of-a-kind, and no one else will have the exact same thing. A home full of DIY projects is a home that feels completely unique and special.

There are so many projects that are great for DIY like painting and refinishing furniture, painting a wall or hanging wallpaper, installing simple light fixtures, creating art or building frames, and creating cool holiday decorations. But some jobs need to be hired out to professionals. If your project requires complex electrical work, replacing or moving pipes or ductwork, or adding a heavy material like tile where none was before, I'd suggest calling in the experts. Basically, projects that could burn, flood, or knock down any part of your home are ones to leave to the pros. Jose is very handy and has a wealth of skills when it comes to more complicated stuff, but we still bring in licensed professionals for things that feel too complex or dangerous. Safety is worth paying for, especially when it comes to your home.

List the projects you have in mind right now:

....

....

Do you have any DIY projects that are languishing and need just a few hours or days to get checked off the list? How can you prioritize those?

....

....

....

Which projects need professionals?

....

....

....

Which do you feel confident you could DIY?

....

....

....

Which are you on the fence about?

....

....

....

If you don't feel confident about whether you can DIY something, do a little research. Read and watch a *few* different articles and videos because you should consider more than one person's opinion when it comes to how doable a project it is. Everyone has different skills, so what looks easy when a pro does it could be too challenging for you. If you give it a try and mess up, it isn't the end of the world. You can always call in a pro to help you fix your mistakes and finish the project, but you'll never know if you can do it if you don't give it a real try!

No. 83 Small Projects

When I say *small projects*, I do mean *small* projects. Don't start your first DIY by laying down a house's worth of hardwood floors or trying to redo your plumbing yourself. Start with sewing your own throw pillow cover from a tea towel or painting a sideboard or antiquing a mirror. Then move up from there.

What DIYs have you wanted to try for a while?

Now, let's prioritize and pick one to three to do in the next few months. If you are ready to try your hand at DIY, here are some tips I think will help:

- Research before you pick up a tool or brush. Do a little Internet searching, read articles, watch videos, and skim through product reviews. Make sure you understand the steps involved and in which order to do them. Double-check that you've purchased the tools, paint, and other materials that will work for your project.
- Make sure you have a clear vision for what you'd like to create. It's more difficult to make decisions if you don't know what you want the finished product to look like.
- Manage your time. Think through how long each step will take, add thirty minutes to your estimate, and then set yourself up for success by setting aside enough time to do that step.

Allow time for drying and curing.

- Don't start a project in the evening that you want to finish that day. You'll be working until the small hours of the morning, cursing yourself as you try to finish. And it won't be your best work because you'll be exhausted.
- Avoid starting projects around holidays or other big days. Do not—I repeat, *do not*—decide to wallpaper your dining room the week before Thanksgiving. *Do not* decide your fireplace needs a coat of paint or fresh mortar three nights before Christmas. *Do not* decide you need new landscaping a week before your annual Easter egg hunt. A month prior to a big day gives you enough time to complete smaller projects, but I wouldn't suggest starting anything later than that. The stress of hosting a holiday coupled with DIY project stress will *not* make for a cozy holiday.
- Let go of perfect. You aren't a machine, and your work won't ever look like it was mass-produced. Focus on making it look good to *you*, even if it isn't completely perfect. No one will notice the imperfections, and "finished and good enough" is always better than "unfinished because it's not perfect."
- Ask for help if you are stuck or unsure. Call your parents, invite over your handy friend for advice, crowdsource online, or ask the people who work at the hardware store. Don't give up; just ask for advice.
- And sometimes, ignore other people's opinions. Advice on technique or how to use a tool or how to fix a mistake is all well and good, but ignore people's unsolicited opinions about your project, especially in the middle of the process. (Everything is messy in the middle, so no judgment allowed.) Focus on what *you* like, what *you* think looks great, and *your* vision for the project. That's what matters because *you* are the one who will be living with it.

NO. 84 Big Projects

When you take on a big project, one of the most important things you can do is to break it down into smaller steps or phases. It can feel difficult to wrap your brain around projects that affect so many aspects of your life (kitchens and bathrooms!), but if you can break down the project into smaller chunks, it might feel easier to make big decisions a little at a time. And once you make some choices, it becomes easier to move on to the next project. Soon the whole thing comes together.

You can break down a project by the order in which things need to happen. That means many cosmetic decisions get left until the final part of the project, and you can adjust these decisions if something else goes over budget. You can also break a project down by:

- What's most important to you
- What's most urgent
- What is necessary
- What would be nice to have

For example, in a bathroom you may feel strongly that adding tile to the ceiling and putting in brass hardware are the two things that are most important to you, but replacing some pipes and a cracked bathtub are the most urgent, new cabinets and countertops are necessary, and new mirrors and light fixtures would be nice to have if they fit in the budget. When you break down the project this way, it helps you decide your priorities and shows where you need to focus on saving and splurging. In this example, I'd pick the tile and hardware first and base my other decisions like the color and shape of the bathtub, the color and style of the cabinets, and the countertop material on those two most important things.

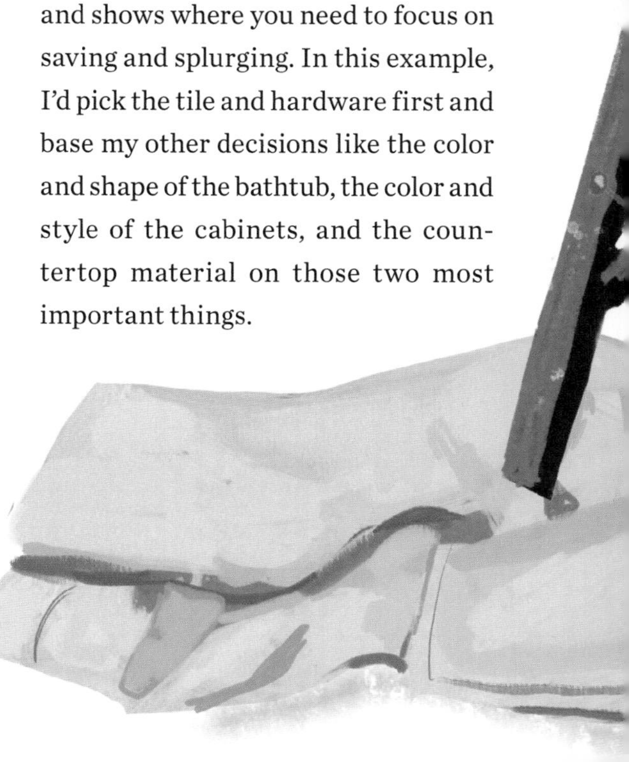

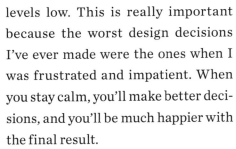

No matter how you break up a project, you still have to deal with the mess and chaos it brings. Our rule for big projects is that as long as we have a bedroom to sleep in, one bathroom to use, and a way to make basic meals and wash dishes, we can stay put. However, if we lose any of those three, we know it's time to book a short-term rental or crash with friends and family until those things are available in our home again. Trust me on this: living through a reno for months without a working shower is not doable!

Another important sanity-saver is to pare down what you have to essentials and get those items very organized. When you are limited to a small portion of your home, the amount of stuff you have out can feel like too much. Packing away anything unnecessary and organizing the things you need will help keep your frustration levels low. This is really important because the worst design decisions I've ever made were the ones when I was frustrated and impatient. When you stay calm, you'll make better decisions, and you'll be much happier with the final result.

Big projects aren't always fun to plan for or live through, but they make a big impact on the coziness level of your home. And oftentimes, especially if you are updating an older home, these kinds of projects are necessary. So do your best to stay calm, organized, and focused on what's most important to you. Trust me, you'll make it through to enjoy the final result!

No. 85

November Home Maintenance Checklist

November is the start of the holiday season at our house, so many of the items on my list for this month are things that will prepare my home for the upcoming festivities. I clean out and restock my pantry with cold-weather essentials and the nonperishable items I know I'll need for making family meals at Thanksgiving and Christmas. That process always reminds me to add a few extra items to my shopping list and drop them off at the food bank for others who may need a little help this season.

NOVEMBER HOME MAINTENANCE CHECKLIST						
	Test your smoke detectors and carbon monoxide detectors. Refresh batteries, if needed. If any of these items are more than seven years old, it's time to replace them!					
	Check your attic for ventilation issues, holes, mold, and pests like rodents or bugs.					
	Make sure all major home appliances are in good working order before the holidays and schedule repairs early this month if needed. The last thing you want is for your oven to go out when cooking the Thanksgiving turkey or your refrigerator to stop working when filled with supplies for Christmas morning breakfast!					
	Clean out the pantry. Toss anything that has expired and set aside anything you don't want that's still good to take to your local food bank.					

	Restock the pantry with nonperishable options you'll need for making soups, stews, roasts, and other cozy cold-weather favorites.					
	Stock up on gasoline, batteries, hand warmer packs, and other winter storm necessities like bottled water, canned goods, and other no-power food options.					
	Stock up on ice melt and kitty litter for walkways. Make sure your snow shovels and ice scrapers are in good working order.					
	If you have a generator, check to make sure it is in good working order in case of power outages from winter storms.					
	Get out your snow blower and other snow-specific equipment like sleds and skis. Make sure they work and have them serviced and fueled if necessary.					
	Put away Halloween décor and replace it with options that have a harvest feel for Thanksgiving.					
	Clean the garbage disposal.					
	Check your HVAC filters and change them as needed.					
	Vacuum your dryer's lint trap.					
	Check your water softener system.					
	Check the temperature on your water heater.					
	If you have pets, give them their monthly flea, tick, and heart guard medicines.					

No. 86 Get Inspired

Building a cozy life and home for yourself won't always be simple. Things that seemed perfectly cozy in the store won't feel that way at home. Sometimes you'll take a risk on a project and hate it. Or you'll just get tired and feel stuck.

My best advice is to rest instead of giving up. Take a break and focus on doing things you love. It's tough to stay inspired when you are tired and overwhelmed with decisions and projects. Take care of yourself and check out mentally so your brain can have a rest too.

You may be surprised at how quickly you find inspiration again if you are willing to look outside the box. Sign out of social media. Instead, go on a home tour, pick up a home magazine you've never read, or go to the library and check out actual design books. Visit historical homes in your area. Watch movies that feature stunning design. Head to art museums and galleries. Check out shops that you've overlooked. Spend some time in nature. Take a creative class. Hang out with your family. Read a great book. Notice what you feel drawn to and lean into things that feel exciting or energizing. That's where you'll find inspiration and motivation for the next phase.

What are some things you always love doing?

....

....

Is there somewhere you go to feel inspired?

....

....

Is there somewhere you've always wanted to visit nearby—a museum, a historic site, a gallery?

....

....

....

What are some activities that always make you feel energetic?

....

....

....

Are there any books you've been wanting to read?

....

....

....

What are your favorite activities to do with your family?

....

....

....

Is there a class you'd like to take?

....

....

....

Are there any cute little shops or boutiques in town that you've never visited? Could you take your mom or a friend with you on a fun date?

....

....

NO. 87 Rest, Refocus, and Shake Things Up

When you get stuck, sometimes you need to give your subconscious time to work in the background. Instead of focusing on what you can't figure out, focus on something completely different. I like to watch a movie, read a book, or play silly games with Cope. Heading out on a fun family outing or a date with your sweetheart is a great ways to redirect your thoughts and give yourself a break. Trust that your brain is still working, even if you aren't actively thinking about whatever had you stuck.

Shake up your routine. Add in more fun. Add in more rest. Add in more play and self-care. We often get stuck when we start to feel burnt out, and that's a huge signal that things are out of balance in your life. As humans we crave that balanced feeling. We want work balanced with play. Rest balanced with activity. Fun balanced with responsibility. Like winter balances summer and spring balances fall, we need to balance our own seasons throughout each year. We can't feel cozy when we get out of whack.

Has your life felt balanced lately?

What is taking up an outsized amount of time and energy for you?

Does it have you feeling stuck?

How can you bring more balance?

What do you feel you need to make more space for in your life right now?

How can you shake up your schedule to add more of what you need?

NO. 88 FAVORITE DATES AND OUTINGS

Outings are one of the best ways to create cozy memories and should be a part of everyone's schedules. They add play and inspiration to our lives, but we have to be intentional about scheduling them.

With Your Spouse

- Dinner at your favorite spot—the one where the food is always good, the ambience is cozy, and it never fails to feel romantic
- A trip to the movie theater with a big bucket of popcorn to share in the dark
- A stroll through a museum to pick out art you'd take home if you had millions to spend
- Going antiquing for new décor and spotting the wild, weird, and crazy things you always find in those shops
- Night swimming under the stars after the kids are in bed
- __________
- __________
- __________
- __________
- __________
- __________
- __________
- __________

As a Family

- Going to the zoo to see all the animals, ride the carousel, and enjoy sticky handfuls of cotton candy
- A trip to the library for story time and a bag of new-to-you books mixed in with old favorites
- A trip to local gardens or arboretums for a picnic in the sunshine and plenty of room to run and play
- A day at the local pool, splashing and swimming
- Hiking or playing at a local park or nature preserve
- ______________________________
- ______________________________
- ______________________________
- ______________________________
- ______________________________

With Your Friends

- A night out for tapas and dancing to good local music
- Brunch on an outdoor patio
- A game night complete with snacks and a silly (but competitive!) spirit
- A day on the lake with a rented boat for tubing, skiing, and floating in the water
- ______________________________
- ______________________________
- ______________________________
- ______________________________
- ______________________________

No. 89 Have Faith

The best thing I can do for myself in every area of life is to feed my soul through time with God. He is the ultimate Giver of peace and joy, warmth and love—all the cozy things. He has blessed me beyond measure, and starting my day thanking Him for all He has given me always puts a smile on my face. My days are better when I spend time with Him in prayer and reading His Word.

I know what it's like to struggle with God because of pain, doubts, and difficult circumstances—if you're in a similar situation, my heart is with you. You aren't alone. I've been there, especially when it felt like God was never going to answer my most fervent prayer. I wanted to be a mother for as long as I can remember, and I prayed for years without an answer from God. I got angry. I had doubts. I felt lost and alone. At times, I felt faithless. But I kept praying and holding out hope that He would say yes, and eventually He did. It didn't look like what I had imagined, and it certainly wasn't on the timeline I'd planned for, but God gave me the perfect little boy to make me a mama. As painful as the journey was, the answer to that prayer was worth every bit of pain and waiting.

Over the years, God has shown up for me time and again. He has held me through the darkest nights, pushed me forward when I would have held back (and missed out), and led me to the opportunities I needed. He has never steered me wrong, and life with Him is so much better. Even if you aren't *sure* how you feel about God, or even if you believe He's there, try saying a prayer. Try talking to Him and letting Him in. You have everything cozy and wonderful and lovely to gain and nothing to lose.

How do you feel about God?

....

....

....

Why? What has shaped that feeling?

....

....

Do you pray regularly?

....

....

What is your favorite verse or inspirational quote?

....

....

....

....

Why does it speak to you?

....

....

....

....

No. 90

December Home Maintenance Checklist

I try to keep my maintenance tasks light during December. It's such a busy month with so many chances to make cozy memories that I want to soak up that time with my family and do a little less around the house.

	DECEMBER HOME MAINTENANCE CHECKLIST					
	Decorate for the winter holidays.					
	Replenish firewood stock if you use a wood-burning stove or fireplace.					
	Check the basement for leaks during thaws.					
	Regularly inspect the roof, gutters, and downspouts for damage after storms.					
	Inspect electrical cords for wear, especially extension cords you may be using for holiday décor!					
	Clean the garbage disposal.					
	Check your HVAC filters and change them as needed.					
	Vacuum your dryer's lint trap.					
	Check your water softener system.					
	Check the temperature on your water heater.					
	If you have pets, give them their monthly flea, tick, and heart guard medicines.					

No. 91 Cozy Planning

Now that you've made it through most of this book and thought about what *cozy* means to you, it's time to start taking those ideas from the page and into your home. The best way to do that is to identify your own cozy style.

Revisit the mood boards you made earlier, whether on Pinterest or somewhere else. Look at each board as a whole and start putting what you see into words you can use to define your style.

What do those images have in common?

....

....

....

Do you see similar colors or specific arrangements? Are you drawn to the same types of lighting, furniture, or décor?

....

....

....

Which elements or pieces are you drawn to over and over?

....

....

....

How would you describe the overall style or blend of styles shown on each board?

....

....

....

How would you *not* describe the style on each board?

....

....

....

What is cozy about all of these images to you?

....

....

....

No. 92 Matching Plans with Spaces

With your mood boards pulled up on your phone or tablet—or from page 41 in this book—walk through your home, room by room. Compare each room to the board you created. This will help you figure out what you need to do, what you don't, and which rooms are the biggest priorities for you.

How does the board match your room?

....

....

Are there elements in your room that are a similar style as the images you pinned?

....

....

How can you get your room closer to what you have pinned on your board? Paint? Small projects? Big projects?

....

....

....

What do you have that's a big departure? Which elements need to be edited out or removed from the room?

....

....

....

What items do you love in each room, and why do you want to keep them?

....

....

....

Which, if any, rooms match your cozy style without needing much work?

....

....

....

Do you have a specific room that really needs some work? Which one, and why?

....

....

How can you create a cozy spot in each of your rooms?

....

....

No. 93 Cast a Vision

Now that you've gathered inspiration and assessed each room, it's time to start envisioning what you really want for your home. Close your eyes and imagine walking around in each and every room. It's your exact house but different—more *you*. You feel cozy and at peace. What do you see when you look around?

What does your dream cozy home look like?

How has your home changed?

Which changes from reality are most exciting to you?

Why does this feel cozier than your current décor?

Is there a specific room that changed the most in your imagination? Which one, and why?

....

....

Which room in your imagination feels especially cozy?

....

....

How do you feel about the changes you'd need to make to go from current to cozy?

....

....

What do you think it would cost?

....

....

What's stopping you from getting started?

....

....

Look at the things that are holding you back. If your answer says anything about making mistakes or failing, know that you aren't alone. We're all afraid of that. And you will make mistakes, or you'll try something and you won't love it as much as you thought you would. That has happened to me more times than I can count. But so many of those home décor failures were easy to fix. You can always repaint or change wallpaper or swap out a light fixture. Yes, it's work to fix things, but it's work worth doing to create a home you love.

No. 94 Own Your Style

Trends come and go, but knowing your personal style is invaluable. Every one of us is so different. You can admire lots of styles and designs and play with trends, but as long as you make selections through the lens of *your* personal style, you will always feel cozy. There are many designers I like who have similar styles to my own. But at the end of the day, our homes look very different because we are all drawn to different things within that style we share. And that's a beautiful thing. It would be terribly boring if we all liked and chose the same things. In case no one ever told you, you have permission to love what *you* love.

As I explained *way* earlier in this book, I'd describe my style as Cozy White Cottage Farmhouse. Whenever I see a new project I'd like to try, or some beautiful wallpaper or a gorgeous sideboard, I ask myself, *Is this Cozy White Cottage Farmhouse?* If it's not, then I know I can admire it, but I don't try to make something fit that won't make me feel cozy.

Of course, sometimes I ask, *Is this the next evolution of Cozy White Cottage Farmhouse?* That's because my style has grown, changed, and evolved over time, and I know it will continue to do so—and so will yours. But I do know my style won't suddenly become Post-Abstract Industrial Chic. It's more likely that it will become Cozy White Cottage Farmhouse 2.0 as a new season of my life ushers in a new love for different (but still muted or neutral) colors, more print and pattern, or new materials. Chances are that your style evolution will be similar—the foundation will stay the same, but the details may change from time to time.

So lean in to your style, whatever it is, and *own it* in your home. You are the one who lives there, so why not go crazy with what you love? You want black walls to fit your Gothic sensibility? Paint them black. Want

shiplap everywhere for the ultimate farmhouse look? Install it. Want to put in crystal chandeliers everywhere and fill your home with pink furniture to create your very own Barbie Dreamhouse? Go for it! I'll be cheering you on because I'm a fan of finding your own cozy and embracing it to create a more peaceful, more comfortable, *more perfectly you* life.

NO. 95 CONNECT WITH NATURE

No matter how cozy we make our homes, nothing can replicate the feeling of the sun shining down on our faces and the breeze blowing through our hair. Getting outside and connecting with nature can be so good for our bodies and our souls.

Stepping away from the screens and artificial lights that dominate our world helps my stress levels and has so many other benefits. If you'd like to take some small steps to help your overall well-being, I highly recommend adding some daily habits to connect yourself with nature.

Here are a few suggestions to help you connect:

- Go for a walk outside. Sometimes this is an exercise walk by myself, and sometimes it's a leisurely stroll with my family. Both recharge and refuel me.
- Care for your indoor plants.
- Take care of your pets. (And when this gets me outside to play with the dogs or feed the sheep, even better!)
- Read on the porch. (Bonus points if it's raining.)
- Do some yoga or stretching on the deck.
- Go for a swim.
- Play in the snow.
- Tend your garden or outdoor plants.
- Spend some time at your favorite outdoor space, and eat a meal alfresco.
- Go for a bike ride.

I've also discovered that finding ways to enjoy different kinds of seasons helps me stay positive and have good days, even if it's not my favorite type of weather.

What are your favorite ways to connect with nature?

....

....

....

....

What things would you like to add?

....

....

....

....

No. 96 Get Ready Every Day

Whether or not you're a morning person, my number-one tip to get your day started on the right foot is to get up and get ready. We all have sick days, and we all need a Saturday morning to lounge around. But for the rest of the time, I really encourage you to create some morning habits that help you feel ready for your day. I find there's something cozy and comforting about a morning routine, and it helps me to be more productive.

I like to get up in time to have an hour to myself in the morning. I drink my coffee, take my time getting ready, and try to do a little reading or praying. I get on the computer and check my messages to ease into a little bit of work. I've never been a morning person, and I've found this alone time helps my day run more smoothly.

"Getting ready" might look a little different for all of us, but I think setting aside time to prep for the day helps us get going. That might be full makeup and heels or sweatpants and gym shoes. Whatever it is for you, find a way to make it cozy and something you look forward waking up to each day.

My favorite morning routine:

1. My morning starts the previous evening, when I plan my next day. I review items on the calendar from meetings to deadlines, and I identify what I want to work on, share on socials, and other general ideas that may impact the next day.
2. I wake up and get coffee.
3. I listen to a podcast or Instagram live post while I get ready.
4. I review the day's plan I made the night before.
5. Then, it's time to get dressed and ready!
6. At this point, I'm reheating my coffee . . .
7. And then I'm ready to execute my day.

Are you a morning person? What does "getting ready" for the day look like for you? Is there something you need to change about your mornings?

Your morning goals for a cozy start to your day:

1. ....
....
2. ....
....
3. ....
....
4. ....
....
5. ....
....

No. 97 Create a Family Mission Statement

Over the years, Jose and I have found that the best way to get where we want to be is to be intentional about it. First, we remember who we want to be and what we want to do. One thing that has helped us live with more intention is creating a family mission statement.

You may want to spend a few days thinking about a potential mission statement and discussing it with your family. Talk about what you value together and what your goals are. What kind of family do you want to be? What do you want to do together? How do you want to make the world a better place together?

Talk, share, ask questions, and then write up your personal mission statement. Record your final version here and return to it when you need some comfort, when you're faced with a decision, or when you are making a big life change. This statement will help you remember who you are and will become a North Star as you navigate the choices you make as a family.

Our home is our happy place.

Our Family Mission Statement

No. 98 Soothing Bedtime Routines

Rest is so important. But sometimes I feel like it's the first thing to get dropped when life gets busy or stressful. Let's spend a couple of days talking about rest and prioritizing that for ourselves and our families. Getting good sleep and allowing our bodies rest is one of the most important things we can do for physical and mental health. I know we could all agree that a great night's sleep is the *epitome* of cozy.

First, I find it helpful to have a bedtime routine. The nights I work late or go to bed in a rush aren't nearly as soothing as nights I'm intentional about getting ready for bed. Here's my ideal evening after reading stories and tucking Cope into bed. I like to bookend my day by ending it in the same way it started.

1. I typically turn on another Instagram live post or podcast.
2. I take a warm bath or shower and put on some cozy pajamas.
3. I love to incorporate some specialty self-care into my bedtime routine. I rotate through face masks, a mani-pedi, bathroom reorganization, a hair mask, or a special healthy snack.
4. I complete my regular nightly skincare routine.
5. I do some light floor stretching or band exercises to get my muscles and body relaxed before bed.
6. And finally, I take my nighttime vitamins and climb into bed.

If you can, I recommend saving up for a comfortable mattress, quality sheets and pillows, and comfortable bedding, as the quality of our sleep is so crucial to our well-being.

Spend some time journaling about your sleep and rest habits and how you can make this a healthier, cozier part of your life.

Cozy Tip

I make skincare a priority because I think it's important for skin health, and I also find it calming. It is, however, very personal. Our skin needs are all different. What works for me may not work for you. If you don't have a routine you love, consider researching some products to enhance your evening skincare.

No. 99 Restorative Rest

Confession: I don't always rest well. My mind is so busy with ideas and to-do lists that I don't allow myself the rest that fuels my body, mind, and soul. I go from one thing to the next, with no margin in between.

I know I'm not the only one. But it doesn't need to stay this way. We can create new habits to get meaningful, restorative rest. Here are a few things I'm implementing in my life that you might also find useful:

1. Take a day off with no agenda. Rest, reflect, and connect with nature and your people.
2. Engage in morning and evening routines that set up your day for success and allow time to wind down.
3. Don't overbook your schedule. It's okay to say no and cut things from the calendar.
4. Walk away from screens. Cut down excess screen time, especially before bedtime.
5. Consider taking a Sabbath day each week.
6. Plan a vacation or staycation. Plan some strategic time off, particularly before or after seasons of stress or busyness.

I'm still a work-in-progress in this area, but it's so important. Reflect on how you can try to rest well.

What are some things you need to cut out of your schedule?

....

....

....

....

....

....

....

How well do you sleep at night?

....

....

....

....

....

....

....

What days or times do you currently have set aside for rest?

....

....

....

....

....

....

....

No. 100 A Practice of Gratitude

Friend, thank you for joining me on this journey to create a cozy home and life. If there's anything I've learned by now, it's that life is filled with highs and lows. There are a lot of things outside our homes that we can't control, but there are a lot that we *can* control inside our homes. And cultivating cozy is the way I create a life and home that I love.

When I stay in my cozy routines, I feel more prepared to handle the hard times and stay present for the good ones. For me, the cozy routines that help me most are keeping my home tidy, feeding my body with nourishing foods, prioritizing exercise, spending time with my family, and filling my soul with rest. I don't always get it right, but just trying to put these routines into place matters so much.

I'm going to leave you with one more cozy tip. It may seem common, but I think it can be an important addition to a cozy life: I want you to practice gratitude often. If you can, try to make it part of every single day.

There are lots of ways to give thanks for the good things in your life. You can write them, think them, or say them out loud. You could absolutely pray about them, especially if you spend some time with God. Go big and broad or small and ordinary. But either way, take a few minutes and let your mind think about every bit of goodness around you. Here's the start of my list:

- My family. This may seem obvious, but I think it's powerful to say it out loud. I'm so thankful for every single person in my family. They absolutely mean the world to me.
- Our farm. I love being able to roam around the beautiful land we have with Cope and Jose and our animals. The way we get to connect with nature, to care for our animals, and to cultivate this little piece of the earth is such a gift.
- And you! I am so thankful for you. Thank you for inviting me into your home and into your life. Thank you for spending some time with me in this book and in my corner of the Internet. I hope this time together has brought joy to your home and helped you and your people in some way.

My Gratitude List

farok
A ROUEN,
AU BUREAU DU JOURNAL, RUE SAINT-LO, N° 7;
ET CHEZ TOUS LES LIBRAIRES DE LA VILLE.
P. COR
COMMENTAIRES,
TOME
Memoir 15 N. Y. State Museum

ESTATE EMULSION
CARD ROOM GREEN No.79
ESTATE EMULSION
WIMBORNE WHITE No.239
ESTATE EMULSION
LICHEN No.19
Plate 66
EFFINGHAM • Barkley Sound • Briny
FRENCH KISS • Miramichi Ba
GEORGES RIVER
GLIDDEN POINT • Damarisc
SPINNEY CREEK • Mai
L'Abbé

Cozy Home Guide

MEASUREMENTS

KITCHEN:

LIVING ROOM:

BEDROOM 1:

BEDROOM 2:

BEDROOMS 3+:

BATHROOM 1:

BATHROOM 2+:

OTHER:

PAINT COLORS, STAIN, AND FLOORING

PAINT BRANDS, COLORS, AND LOCATIONS

STAIN COLORS, TYPES, AND LOCATIONS

FLOORING MANUFACTURERS, TYPES, AND LOCATIONS

FABRICS

NOTES:

SWATCHES:

About the Author

Liz Marie Galvan is a bestselling author, blogger, mama, wife, and co-owner of the home décor boutique The Found Cottage. Liz blogs daily on her website, LizMarieBlog.com, where thousands of people go for tips and inspiration each day—whether she's blogging about life on the farm, their fixer-upper 1800s farmhouse, her latest DIY project, or even about their adoption journey. Liz lives in Michigan with her veteran husband, Jose, and their son, Copeland Beau, along with a few sheep, a lot of bees, a bunch of cats, and even a couple of dogs. Other books by Liz include *Cozy White Cottage*, *Cozy White Cottage Seasons*, and *We Belong to Each Other* (a children's book). You can follow Liz and all of her adventures on Instagram @LizMarieGalvan.